Thomas Sheridan is an author, artist and filmmaker from Dublin, Ireland who came to international recognition in 2011 with the book *Puzzling People: the Labyrinth of the Psychopath*. In the years since, he has written several more books, and has made films on topics such as social engineering, political and corporate pathology, and on to the occult foundations surrounding the emerging years of the *Third Reich*. In recent times, his work into ancient mysteries and locations has been featured in some of the world's largest media outlets, and he is a highly sought-after public speaker around the world.

www.streetdruid.net
www.thomassheridanarts.com

Published by Street Druid and ThomasSheridanArts

First Edition

ISBN: 978-0-244-36414-4

Cover Artwork by Kati Williams
All interior illustrations are in the *Public Domain* or are the work of the author himself.

MAGIC HAS GONE THE WAY OF
ROMANTIC INTIMACY. BROADCASTED
TO THE WORLD AND THE POWER OF
THE EXPERIENCE IS GONE.

SORCERY MUST BE SECRETIVE
AND PRECIOUS...

SORCERY

The Invocation of Strangeness

THOMAS SHERIDAN

ON BECOMING VISIBLE AND INVISIBLE

It was a beautiful Spring day, in which the sky above me was lavishly decorated with gigantic white clouds sweeping in from the Atlantic Ocean. Towering, levitating white mountains of vapor. All perfectly punctuating the cobalt and cerulean-coated endless vista above and behind them. The landscape around me, itself, was coming to life once again. As the iridescent, emerging green leaf buds of the hawthorn bushes moved slowly out from their protective branches—which had generated them into manifestation—and out towards another recommencing of the natural and unstoppable cycles of life, death and rebirth.

I stood atop the suitably 'cyclopean' architecture of the five-thousand-year-old Creevykeel megalithic site. Gazing out past the Gothic edifice of Classiebawn castle, and out beyond that again, towards the vast ocean, it was then that the full meaning of the term 'sorcery' found a suitable level of cognitive equilibrium within my conscious awareness. Within magic, there is no moral stance, nor ethical objectivity. All energy is neutral at the starting point of zero. Therefore, all magic and sorcery is without objectivity at the initial point of charge. If we can imagine it, we can conjure it, and the results will be as surprising and fantastical as the initial desire to bring the non-material into manifestation. What we get is not what we want, but rather, what we need. Sorcery is the ultimate feedback loop between consciousness and the cosmos. Who and what we are will ultimately be what we conjure.

While standing atop the ancient Creevykeel edifice, I practically had to restrain myself from reciting *Ye Adjuration of the Great Cthulhu,* as I beheld the timeless profundity of the surrounding landscape before me. If I had not been escorting a tour group at the time, I am almost certain that I would have turned my attention toward the ocean and called out:

"In His House at R'lyeh Dead Cthulhu waits dreaming..."

I can think of no better way to convey the concept of my own personal relationship towards sorcery than how I felt on that tranquil Spring afternoon surrounded by megaliths, magic and mythology. Here I was, acting like a high priest or shaman—standing atop thousands of years of ancient masonry in the form of a Neolithic monument—summoning a fictional aquatic-bound cosmic entity created by the American science fiction and fantasy writer H.P. Lovecraft back in 1928. Cthulhu may be a fictional character, but one which—in the years since Lovecraft's death in 1937—has for millions of people (including myself) become something approaching that of a very real creation.

Yet, was my invocation of the great Cthulhu any less authentic than the past ceremonial rites issued forth by the original shamans, druids—and, dare I say it, magical sorcerers—who in the far-off past stood atop the same stones and invoked their own gods thousands of years previously? Apart from accepting the guilt of my own (slightly) sacrilegious trespass upon the location, the answer is no. The most powerful gods possible are the ones which we create for ourselves.

It matters not if the great Cthulhu is actually dead and dreaming at the bottom of the ocean, or merely within the pages of some books I first read as a teenager. The actual physical manifestation of the monsters and supernatural beings within Lovecraft's *Promethean* worldview is irrelevant to the authenticity that the experience—the *Cthulhu Mythos*—generates within the mindscape of the great many people who admire Lovecraft's writings. Amid the consciousness of millions of intelligent, educated and rational people the world over, Cthulhu and the other *Elder Gods* are as real to them as Jesus Christ is to a Christian, or Allah is to a Muslim. Lovecraft—along with the mythos he created around a gigantic, humanoid-looking, octopus-dragon hybrid he named Cthulhu—is indeed very real within the full, holistic sense of how these humans experience their own engagement within this five sense reality. This 'reality' of Cthulhu has arisen by means of well-written and believable literature. One which even comes complete with its own symbolism-laden magical grimoire known as the *Necronomicon*.

In today's world, the Lovecraftian mythos has become a global sensation. There is an entire industry of games, merchandise, and even actual conjuration texts devoted to the summoning of various Lovecraftian entities from Yog-Sothoth to Shub-Niggurath—as well as the other *Elder Gods*—into this reality. Which, I might add, several occultists claim to have successfully achieved. I believe them. Why wouldn't I believe them? Lovecraft's mythos is real because human consciousness is capable of making it real. Just as previous occultists in the past had summoned the *Titans* of ancient Greece, or the *Guardian Angels* of Christianity during their own magical invocations.

These entities represent visualizations of archetypal energy forces particular to man and his experience of the universe. Invent some gods (or demons) of your own—if the Archangel Michael or Cthulhu does not appeal to you—and you'll conjure them, too. If your focus, concentration and *Will* is determined enough to make it happen, it will happen. Lovecraft himself was a complex, tormented and tortured man who was the epitome of the cosmos providing such an individual with what they needed, and not what they specifically desired. That being—in the case of Lovecraft—the supernaturalized legitimacy of his own artistic output. The same supernatural world which he vehemently denied even existed. As a result of the entities and beings which had communicated with Lovecraft during his dreaming, he became what he claimed to ridicule. From this passive invocation, they entered into his fictional writing, and then he released them into the world. Lovecraft himself became the magician he had spent a lifetime attempting to deny.

On that day in which I stood looking out over the vastness of the Atlantic Ocean, I would have not been in the least surprised if the great Cthulhu's gargantuan bulk had actually begun to emerge from out of the waters of Sligo Bay. That is, if I had actually attempted to invoke him with an incantation. Naturally, I am talking in metaphors...for now. Or am I?

WHEN CTHULHU WHISPERED FROM THE ABYSS

In 1997, hydrophones across the Pacific Ocean recorded a loud, ultra-low frequency sound which was picked up by the *National Oceanic and Atmospheric Administration*'s numerous listening stations thousands of miles apart. The mysterious sound became known as the *Bloop*, and it was initially determined to be organic in nature. Eventually, a seismologist from an American university was brought forward to claim that the sound was created by an ice quake in Antarctica. Yet, apart from a single sound bite in *Wired* magazine, no other proof of this being the cause of the strange sound was ever presented. As usual, when the supernatural becomes too close to reality, any scientific excuse will suffice.

What made the *Bloop* particularly interesting is that the epicenter of the sound was discovered to be in the area of the Pacific where Lovecraft had determined his fictional Cthulhu waits dead, and dreaming. Not surprisingly, thousands of Lovecraft fans from all over the world—mostly with tongues firmly in cheek—excitedly stated it was Cthulhu waking from his dreaming, to once again walk upon the earth, so as to destroy the human mind within a maelstrom of madness and psychic implosion.

CROWLEY'S 'NESSIE' AND LOVECRAFT'S CTHULHU

Understandably, their excitement can be somewhat forgiven when one considers that there is evidence to suggest that the *Loch Ness Monster* itself was created as a result of a magical ritual which Aleister Crowley had performed in 1889. Crowley began—but left unfinished—his working of the rite of *Abra-Melin the Mage* from his home at Boleskine House by the shores of Loch Ness. A water elemental arose—accidentally created by Crowley—which many now consider to be the fabled monster of this Scottish lake. The many-hyped appearances of the *Lough Ness Monster* started to occur **after** Crowley had left the location, due to 'the

Wickedest Man in the World' finding the *Abra-Melin the Mage* ritual far too stressful and intense even for the 'Great Beast 666' himself.

Some would cite, to the contrary, the legend of the Irish missionary Saint Columba—banishing a monster in 565AD—as proof of the *Lough Ness Monster*'s existence prior to Crowley's arrival at Boleskine House. However, due to the paranoia of early Christian missionaries, just about every lake and river in both Ireland and Scotland contained monsters in need of high-profile exorcisms, usually performed in an attempt to impress the local Pagans. On a very mystical level, there is a far deeper symbolism to these aquatic exorcisms. Replace an actual deep lake monster with that of it representing an allegory of the subconscious Pagan soul still residing within the locals. Suddenly, the idea takes on a far more interesting line of speculation. A baptism of the landscape, so to speak, and, by extension, the very personal and tribal Pagan connection towards the landscape itself. It should also be noted that Saint Columba is reputed to have chased a monster out of the River Ness, at a location which is several miles away from the actual loch itself. As usual, the skeptic mind is as ignorant of actual folklore as much as they are ignorant of the power of complex metaphor and archetypes.

Human consciousness is intrinsically linked with bodies of water. Among the depths are keys to salvation and destruction. Regardless of any nervous tittering—or more likely, factually incorrect or baseless debunking—emanating from the skeptics who find comfort in prosaic explanations for such events as the *Bloop*, at least on an energetic level, perhaps everything that Cthulhu's manifestation represents is already happening within the present version of the Western consciousness.

THE AEON OF CTHULHU?

We live in an age where many people's minds do appear to be subject to incremental cognitive annihilation. We are told that many things we have previously believed to be accepted as fact are now to be reordered and reconstructed into a bewildering maelstrom of cultural, political, social and sexual identity paradigms. All of this taking place within a confusing turmoil of social, ethnic and theocratic mass-media hysteria. The Cthulhu that once lay dead, and dreaming—within the depths of the human psyche—does appear to have begun to move up to the surface of the collective consciousness. Which any Jungian worth their salt would be only too quick to recognize and understand.

Lovecraft's sorcery is indeed working. On the psychic level for the time being, Cthulhu is here. Shifts in human consciousness and cultural convulsion have always been complemented with sub-aquatic monsters representing the symbolic depths of the society undergoing these changes. By becoming something of a *Captain Nemo,* exploring these psychic depths beforehand can save you from being consumed by them when they finally emerge. Magic and sorcery affords us this ability.

THE DREAM OF THE MOON AND THE SEA

One night, in the year 2000, I had a dream. In this dream, an ancient and unknown voice spoke to me. I was told that what is presently considered to be human consciousness had once existed at the bottom of the deepest oceans. In order for consciousness to move to the surface of the planet, our collective minds—while still in this deep aquatic state—began to dream the Moon into existence. The Moon's formation had been required in order to regulate natural cycles on Earth, and thereby, allow evolution to wake consciousness up—from its dreaming—within the depths of the darkest seas. In order for this to occur, the Moon had to be a precise size and distance from the Earth. Thus, this is how the dream had informed me—via my subconscious processes—why the Earth came to have such an unusual lunar satellite, relative to the size and position, when compared to the other planets of the *Solar System*.

The voice in the dream informed me that the creation of the Moon was the first act of sorcery undertaken upon this planet. To ensure this great event would never be forgotten—as consciousness rose to the surface to evolve into different life forms—lunar and solar eclipses were created. So as to remind us that when we look up and gaze upon the Moon, this is how we came to be what we are now as a species. I then woke up from this dream and gazed at the bedside clock. The time was 3:33AM. At the zenith of the so-called 'witching hour'. When I got up to go to the bathroom, I looked out of my kitchen window, and there was a sliver of a crescent moon hanging over the Irish Sea. What did this dream actually mean and prove? Everything and nothing, like all strange dreams. However, it did make me pay attention to ideas which I had not been interested in prior to this fantastical nocturnal extravaganza. Something new inside me had been literally switched on. I was not going to take it for granted, nor pass it off as coincidence. Real or not, I had been given an answer to a question concerning the strangeness of the Moon, and one which I had been puzzled by.

SORCERY IS VERY REAL

This book will prove to you that sorcery and magic are very real, and you can yourself learn to use these powers to make your own life more creative, fulfilling and interesting. As a result of learning to understand how the dynamics of sorcery unfolds—as well as learning how to place yourself into magical states of consciousness—you'll become far more creative in your everyday life, and also enjoy a greatly improved version of yourself. This is because you will be fully responsible for the development of your own consciousness, and then, by extension, the unfolding of a far more meaningful and delicious reality than that which you may be presently experiencing around yourself, and within your everyday life.

You will become a magnet, able to attract your desires and wishes more easily. Rather than being merely an iron filing caught within the fluctuations of the exterior electromagnetic and sub-atomic fields, while hoping that you eventually get a favorable charge.

You can create your own charge and direct it as you wish.

Sorcery is more about remembering what you already knew, rather than learning completely new information. Therefore, this book is very much my own personal approach to the topic. An approach that is based upon useful magical practice which I have found invaluable for both the improvement of my own quality of life, as well as my personal creativity. Along with this, one can also develop the skills required to deflect psychic attacks and energy vampirism—both intended and passive—undertaken by others.

I shall include include historical and sociological citations and examples —from the history of sorcery, magic and the occult—so as to create something of a sense of an overall 'magical perception' within the reader. In doing so, this will help the reader come to terms with the effects which sorcery—as well as the occult sciences—have had upon human society and history throughout the ages. A good seventy five percent of becoming a magician or mystic is to observe the everyday world as a symphony of magical happenstances and experiences. This includes your dreaming life which is the realm where magic and sorcery presents feedback data on your psychic state, and also affords the opportunity to move beyond the space-time restrictions of our daily cognitive processes.

BESPOKE AND PERSONAL SORCERY

At the turn of the twentieth century, the British occultist and artist, Austin Osman Spare, proved conclusively that magic can be reconstructed and rebuilt into a personal working model. This is the overall approach that I have also taken within this book. The only risks associated with this holistic, bespoke assemblage of your own personal magical, esoteric and occult smorgasbord is that you may embark upon doing so without fully understanding the basics. As well as not paying suitable homage to the past magical foundations upon which human consciousness presently stands. More importantly, you'll need to fully understand yourself—as well as your own personal reasons—for embarking upon your journey into the world of magic and sorcery.

By 'basics', I am not necessarily referring to any specific archaic or time-tested rites and rituals, per se. I am talking about the very personal relationship each and every one of us has within the underlying—and generally unseen—dynamics of the universe. Which also happens to be the same dynamics of the human consciousness. An idea that was universally accepted and understood in an age long before the Abrahamic religious traditions began moving out of the Middle East and into the rest of the world. The *Book of Enoch*—as told in the *Old Testament*—is as much a story describing the strangulation of the human psyche as it is that of an Abrahamic fanatic at war with the self-autonomy of the people around him. It's time to loosen this grip.

Magical practice, as well as historical examples, information and ideas contained within this book—as with all of my other work—are designed to help you, the reader, create a barrier against the forces which have been masticating upon your soul since the time you were an infant. Robbing you of both your full spiritual—and especially—your creative potential as a human being. For the reader of this book who is willing to follow the text to its completion—while sequestering the ideas and information into their subconscious minds—your mystical *fait accompli* can end now. You do not have to be the person society told you who, and what, you are. You can become the best version of whomever you choose to be. Sorcery is the road map that will lead you towards this psychic and creative proficiency.

Look to the life of many artists for guidance. David Bowie being a good example of someone who built a creative magical road map into an unknown and rich territory. One that he alone discovered. Guided by *Major Tom,* his muse of conjuration. His final *Blackstar* album— particularly the music video for the title track—was a deliberate ritual which literally blasted his spirit into another cosmos. This is why David Bowie does not actually feel 'dead' to us. Bowie used his artistic genius and knowledge of magic to become a literal god. We should all be doing this.

POETIC CONJURATIONS

When people ask me to give them an example of how sorcery actually works, my answer often surprises them. This sense of surprise comes from two factors: firstly, what I tell them is not what they expected to hear. Secondly, how I convey my own particular theory of sorcery often bemuses them. My primary magical objective is to use art and science in order to hack the operating system of the cosmos, so as to make my own life more meaningful. My personal philosophical expressions of magical practices are based heavily upon the concepts developed through my own exploration of *Folk Magic*, *Druidry* and paganism. I carry the sorcery of my ancestors within my DNA. As we all do. Regardless of where we come from.

HOW ANCIENT HUMANS USED SORCERY

Imagine early man observing lightning striking a tree. With what little knowledge he had at the time—due mainly to his non-ending effort to survive from day to day—such early humans would have considered the lightning bolt a transmission of the mysterious solar fire of the Sun down to the Earth. Trees being the repository—or storehouses—of the Sun's life-giving fire. They may have even considered this to be the means by which the forest returns to life at the start of Spring. Then, at some point, an early human rubbed two sticks of wood together, and from doing this, he or she noticed it began to heat up and generate smoke. If he or she blew upon it, it would release the same 'magic fire' from the Sun that had been stored within the tree. Following this incredible feat, our ancient ancestor—ostensibly now a 'magician'—was able to free the solar fire from the wood, so the tribe remained safe during the blackness of the night. At the center of the two sticks—where the friction ignited into a spark—was created the 'light of the world'.

Now just try to consider—on a psychological level—how intense that experience must have been for early humans. The solar god in the Sun—through the arc of lightning—places his offspring into the tree until man 'mates' two sticks together and creates his own fire. It was not only a mere novelty; this 'trick' was also capable of improving and extending life. Added to this, moving human experience into previously unknown realms, to the point whereby the darkest reaches of caves—leading into the Earth's deep interior—could be accessed with the light from the Sun held as flaming torches, to create the first great artworks of the human race. These cave paintings were magical in nature and very often based on totemic concepts of humans taking on the specific attributes of certain animals in order to obtain their powers for hunting and protection. Although these early humans were as intelligent as we are today, it was the application of magical metaphors and allegorical ideas that generated new neural connections within their brains leading to emerging complexities towards both linguistic and aesthetically-minded development. All this came exclusively from sorcery. Sorcery is the process from which all spiritual and scientific ideas arrive. It is the magical fire within us all.

Of course, we know now that early humans, and their mystical rationalization of the fire-making process, is not scientifically true at all. Considering that early man knew nothing of the laws of thermodynamics, climate and cosmology, the use of metaphor created the magical narrative so as to contain the entire experience into a supernatural framework. A supernatural framework which brought a greater and more purposeful meaning beyond the constant struggle for survival. Eventually, these concepts of humanity's special relationship with the solar god—who sleeps in the ocean at night as the Sun sets in the West, leaving man to keep his fire alive during the darkest hour—developed into more ritualistically-specific ideas, as well as regional variations all across the globe.

The so-called *Celtic Cross* symbol—or 'high cross' as it is known in Ireland—with its quadrant circle, is almost certainly initially rooted within the primordial symbolism of humans making fire by rubbing two sticks together. The circle around the cross being the Sun itself, while at the center of the cross is the aforementioned 'light of the world'. An idea that later Christianity—along with many hundreds of Pagan spiritual traditions—would incorporate into their own forms of sorcery, supernatural expression and religion. Within Indo-European tradition, these symbols became powerful magical designs embedded deeply within our collective unconscious minds. A repository of the primordial sorcery of our ancestors. That being, the charging of the solar fire in accordance with *Will*, rather than happenstance. We are hardly going to forget such a monumental event in human history so easily.

Likewise, the *Swastika* would have also been derived from this same concept concerning the symbolism of the invocation of the solar deity. Later refined—and expanded upon—from culture to culture. Although it should be clearly noted that this particular design (and similar motifs) are very much Indo-European in origin. This is especially evident in the symbolism of the *Brigid's Cross*. Ostensibly, the *Swastika* of the Gaels. The Pagan deity upon whom Saint Brigid is based upon (Bríd) is a goddess intrinsically connected to ritualistic traditions of the hearth fire and domestic well-being invoked by means of ceremonial magic. Later, the Christians turned this domestic ceremonial sorcery into prayers and blessings. As with all these Indo-European magic fire/solar symbols, the cardinal points of the compass developed from this association of the four quadrants (North, South, East and West) inherent within the design. Eventually making its way into conceptualizing particular dynamics, or attributes, of the human psyche. What began as rubbing two sticks together eventually (and this is proof positive of the power of magic) became the foundations of marine navigation, and even Jungian psychology. The power of sorcery could hardly be more beautifully portrayed than with this example of magical and archetypal evolution. The mystery of friction—to our ancient ancestors—eventually allowed us to explore the external and internal worlds. *As Above, So Below.* This may well explain why our earliest ancestors took their fire deep into the earth—via vast cave systems—so as to work their magic and invoke their gods. The deeper the 'cave', the more powerful the sorcery.

YOUR WORLD TODAY IS A PRODUCT OF PAST SORCERY

This one example demonstrates just how incredibly ancient the spiritual and religious ideas of today actually are. In fact, one could even make the point—within the general nature of religious tradition—that almost nothing new in terms of ritual has been invented since the times of the earliest humans. It is merely the complexity of the rituals themselves that have become more elaborate. Their on-going development being something of a by-product of human social and cultural evolution. However, regardless of the mystical traditions at their root, they are all extrapolated pageants of very basic Pagan and proto-shamanic magical rituals. The same could be said for both philosophy and psychology.

Did it matter that these early humans—who released the solar fire from the trees—were unaware or ignorant of the actual scientific processes involved in making fire happen? Not at all. Was he or she still creating real sorcery in the truest sense? Absolutely, they were. This is what sorcery is and always will be: the ability to use the presently mysterious forces of the universe—and from these unknown forces—to alter the very nature of reality and the material world as it is presented to us. In the case of making fire; turning night into day, and from this, turning the deepest, darkest caves into the wombs of gods and magical conjuration. It has been like this from the Neanderthal era on. It remains so to the very present, and will continue on regardless of how advanced human scientific discovery becomes.

Until the nature of all the mysterious forces of the cosmos are discovered —along with their complex and profoundly mysterious relationship to human consciousness—all these unknown and unseen forces of the cosmos (as well as that of the human mind) will begin their initial engagement within our consciousness in the form of sorcery. This includes these forces being considered magical gods, goddesses, demons, fairies, djinns, spells, incantations, rituals and other accessible metaphors. Their names and effects being eventually re-branded into scientific theories. Until then, there remains a vast amount of sorcery in the universe waiting to be unleashed.

GROWING UP IN HIDDEN SHADOWS

As I mentioned in my previous book *The Druid Code: Magic, Megaliths and Mythology*, the European magical tradition has been under constant attack by Christians—as well as other Abrahamic cults from the Middle East—for almost two thousand years. This very real psychic war has raged within Western consciousness to the point where today, most Europeans—as well as people of European origin—can hardly imagine a time when their ancestors were not Christians. Although this situation has been slowly swinging back in the other direction in recent times, we still have a long way to go before Europeans have a proper understanding and appreciation for the mystical lives and traditions of their ancestors.

Being from Ireland, I was raised to believe that (the probably fictional) Saint Patrick, almost as soon as he arrived on our shores—sometime in the mid to late fifth century—had instant success in converting the Pagan Irish towards the teachings of the *Church of Rome*. While admittedly, there was something of a troublesome short episode while Saint Patrick was dealing with the 'wickedness' of the 'evil' druids, in no time at all, the entire population of Ireland were soon devote Christians. Delighted—we are told—to have been freed from their insidious heathen culture and superstitions. How Saint Patrick had thankfully replaced them with the more rational ideas of venerating a circumcised Hebrew miracle worker, wandering the desert thousands of miles away. One who was raised from the dead after being nailed to a cross, and who also called himself the 'light of the world'.

Perhaps the very idea of Saint Patrick himself—as a story—was an act of Roman magic? Created in the aftermath of a possibly murderous and suppressed history concerning the converting of the Pagan Irish towards the Roman church. Cleaned up, re-written and without the input of the Pagan Irish themselves and what they may have felt about the loss of their indigenous spiritual worldview.

In no time at all, the lie becomes the truth. *Abracadabra...* The reality is that Christianity may have taken up to a thousand years to establish itself fully in Ireland. As late as the *Renaissance* era, there were reports of rural communities still venerating the Cromm Cruach—the last Pagan god of Ireland—almost one thousand years after the arrival of Saint Patrick. While we may have lost—for a time—the mystical worldview of our ancestors, something in our genetic memories never forgets this. Like honey, it has no shelf life.

OLD SORCERY NEVER DIES

When the *Penal Laws* (between 1660 and 1869) ostensibly made being a Catholic an illegal act in Ireland, people would secretly meet at *Mass*

Rocks to conduct religious services out of sight of the British colonial administration. By the time *Catholic Emancipation* was granted, the rural Irish were involved in a spiritual life surrounding 'sacred rocks' which was hardly much different than that of their Neolithic and Bronze Age Pagan ancestors. Along with these *Mass Rock,* makeshift congregations, a tradition of *Hedge Schools* had also developed, so as to provide the Irish Catholics with the education denied to them by the *Penal Laws.* Classes were held in secret locations, within woodlands and other secluded outdoor places. Students were bonded by secrecy and oaths not to disclose the location of these clandestine, 'invisible' schools. Just as they had been the case in early Christian times, when the druids performed a similar clandestine function with their own teachings.

When Irish Catholics were finally allowed to be formally educated again, it was soon discovered that these *Hedge Schools* had developed into a very high level of educational practice. To the point where former *Hedge School* teachers were soon being sought out—even by Protestants—for their children to be educated by. Such was the reputation these learning institutions had attained. One of these Protestant post-*Hedge School* pupils was John Tyndall, the 19th-century Irish physicist who achieved his renowned scientific credentials through his study of diamagnetism, infrared radiation and the physical properties of air. Tyndall brought scientific experimentation to the masses, and yet his early schooling was based on the same types of education lineage that the druids had provided among their sacred groves thousands of years previously.

Once again, the underlying sorcery of the druids had never vanished. As with their spiritual connection surrounding large stones, the rural Irish also had an instinctual supernatural connection to the natural world. They sought salvation—in all its forms—among the same natural locations that the druids and the previous proto-shamanic traditions had done so before them. Even Tyndall's primary field of diamagnetism—for which he was most celebrated—is a quantum mechanical effect that has been associated with some of the strange forces found at stone circles and other sacred megalithic sites. Tyndall, while being known for his opposition towards organized religion—was nonetheless also something of a mystic—having even been described as a 'magician' by his admirers.

THE SORCERY WITHIN THE SCRIPT

This Christian war against the Irish magical tradition—directly overseen initially by Saint Patrick from this Roman administrative center at Navan Fort—included the destruction of the Pagan Irish usage of the magical writing known as *Ogham* (pronounced 'o-ham'), which is directly related to Pagan earthly and supernatural archetypes. Dozens, if not hundreds, of upright *Ogham* standing stones were attacked—in the classic Christian iconoclastic wild and histrionic fashion—with hammers and other weapons. Many were toppled over on their sides, and had their inscriptions buried out of sight. Others—and this is extremely important to note—had their markings shaped into crucifixes, so as to imply the Christians were in control of Ireland for longer than they actually were.

The same messianic vandalism we associate in the modern world with Islamic sects—such as ISIS destroying the *Temple of Baal* in Syria—also took place in the Nordic world with *Rune* inscriptions, as well as in Ireland and parts of Britain (notably Wales and Cornwall) with the *Ogham* stones. Why would Christian missionaries seek to destroy the ancient Pagan script of European peoples such as that found on the *Ogham* of Ireland, or the *Runes* of the Germanic and Nordic world? The answer is because such texts were much more than mere writing. They were magically inscribed incantations—carved into stone—so the spell they cast would last as long as the stone itself. Therefore, it was paramount for the Christians to destroy or alter them. In the case of *Ogham*, these carved stones were the magical ciphers of the Gaelic tribes. *Sigils* in stone, and their power and symbolism went right back to the rock art of the Neolithic era.

From the time of Saint Patrick to the very present, this vandalism— although these days it is text books, rather than hammers used to deface them—remains part and parcel of academic life in Ireland. The utterly absurd—to the point of laughable—officially-sanctioned mandate that all *Ogham* script is a product of the *Medieval* age still persists in Ireland among academia. These Jesuit-trained professors—as well as church-funded colleges and universities they work for—are still frantically destroying (although on a far more respectable level) the ancient magical tradition of the Irish people. A cursory glance at what is known as *Orthodox Ogham* immediately reveals the magical, shamanic nature of the Gaelic tribes who created them. Inscriptions such as ᴵᴵᴵᴵ⸱⸱⸱ᵀᵀᵀ⸱⸍⸱⸍⸍ᵀᵀ⸱⸱⸱⸱ (*prince of wolves*), or ᵀ⸍⸍⸍⸍⸍⸱ᵀᵀᵀ⸱⸱⸍⸱⸱⸱ᵀᵀᵀ⸱⸱⸱⸱ (*born of raven*), and the profoundly magical ᵀ⸱⸱⸱⸱ᵀᵀ⸱⸱⸱⸱ᴵᴵ⸱⸱ᵀᵀᵀ⸱ᵀᵀᵀ (*alive like fire*), continue to be taught within academic studies as being Christian in origin.

They are clearly conveying universally-accepted totemic sorcery and magical concepts derived from the Pagan consciousness. Much of the earliest surviving *Ogham* script also makes reference to the Celtic solar deity Lugh, as well as constant descriptions relating to the magical attributes of various species of trees. In particular, the oak and the yew. This is Druidry to its very core. Yet, Irish academia still staunchly opposes entertaining any notion that these inscriptions are not pre-Christian in either symbolism or execution. Instead, the official stance is that the ancient Irish were a backward and dangerous people—who had no written language—and certainly had no complex spiritual tradition (of any real depth) until the arrival of Saint Patrick in the 4th century.

Many examples of ancient Irish *Ogham* writings—which could not be burnt in a fire—can still be found, which convey complex mystical and magical ideas. Affirmations of sorcery which at the same time are perfectly correlated to the tales of Irish mythology. These stories and epics are themselves resplendent with complex and deeply magical and mythological motifs. This ruthless, spiritual conquest that took place in Ireland happened everywhere the Abrahamic religions invaded. In particular, with cultures subjected to Christian incursions.

THE PROOF OF SORCERY IS THAT IT STILL EXISTS

The brutal and sadistic murder of Hypatia—during the sacking of the *Library of Alexandria* by fanatical Christians in 415AD—should be considered within the context of an opening salvo and not a terminal event. The fact that any form of sorcery or magical tradition has survived at all—within Western society—is incredible in and of itself, and only serves to demonstrate the power and endurance of the magical tradition.

Magical experiences, as well as occultic agendas—which have taken place during a previous era—have an interesting manner of revealing their craft and effectiveness in the most surprising ways. When, over the course of time, their fulfillment manifests before us. What was once occult—that is, 'hidden' in the truest sense—eventually jumps into our consciousness from the past. Often, in the most poetic and ironic of ways. The original intent, or initial objective of the magical process, tradition or spell, waits patiently—to eventually unfold before our eyes—while the world has long ago lost sight of the sorcerer's existence and intentions. A waiting game akin to a *Jack in the Box* slowly being cranked—out of sight and out of mind—before it jumps suddenly and starkly into our present-day reality.

THE GESTATION OF WILL

This 'waiting game' was precisely what the *'Great Beast 666',* Aleister Crowley himself, allowed to set in motion—when he retired from ritual magical practices in 1923—to work on *The Confessions.* This contained his record of the *Great Revelation of 1904* in Cairo, when the gods made it known to him that he was to be their chosen messenger. Crowley— along with his latest young maiden Hanni—waited in London for the time when he would become the navigator of human destiny. Which Crowley achieved (after his death) due to the enormous influence he had upon the development of popular culture and the emerging social dynamics of the second half of the 20th century. Sorcery needs its own time for it to manifest. It works most effectively when the initial force of the *Will*—at the point of intention—has been completely forgotten within the conscious mind of the magician or witch.

HOUSES OF THE UNHOLY

It was back in 2012, at Number 9/9a Aungier Street—which also happens to be Dublin's oldest remaining house—when a building that was undergoing the process of being converted into apartments, unleashed a surprising discovery. During dendrochronology procedures—that is, testing the wood beams to establish their age—that 'witch marks' connected to the world of *Apotropaic Magic* (the warding off the *evil eye*/curses) were discovered on the second-floor joists. They had been hidden away for hundreds of years. Out of sight and out of mind. Sequestered within the concealed structure of a mundane old domicile of a European capital city. Carved as an inverted '*VV*' or '*M*', it was a reminder of a time when most people sought to ward off evil spirits—or humans with malicious intentions—who may have wished harm to the dwelling, along with the occupants living inside. An even more interesting discovery was uncovered soon afterwards, when a child's shoe (along with a rib bone of a sheep) were located hidden behind the walls in the same room. Their placement strongly suggested that they had been very purposefully entombed within the building—at very specific locations—and for a very magical reason. Occultic in the most truest sense of the term.

The purpose of hiding a child's shoe is derived from a once common *Folk Magic* tradition, well recorded across the Irish Sea in England, at a time when it was believed that children's shoes were considered especially powerful in defending a building from demons, or demonically-possessed humans with malicious intent. More interestingly, the shoe—along with the carved '*VV*' or '*M Apotropaic Magic* marking—were the first of their kind found in Ireland. Significantly, from a time when Puritans were increasing wielding political and social power in both Britain and Ireland. An age when all forms of sorcery were being forbidden, and practitioners of such crafts were being shunned, persecuted or imprisoned, if not executed. At the same time, when the full nature of the artifacts discovered at Number 9/9a on Aungier Street began to reveal themselves—along with their occultic secrets—across the other side of Dublin to the north of the old city and its rapidly extending suburbs, archaeologists uncovered a vast 'magical landscape', which had been hidden below farmland for centuries—and almost completely forgotten about—within a townland known as Bay, a pre-Christian continuous Neolithic, Bronze and Iron Age community, which includes a significant pennannular enclosure, triple-ring barrow, along with some earlier prehistoric mounds which were unearthed.

How such a significant antiquarian landscape could remain undiscovered in Ireland was extremely unusual. Irish folklore and tradition mandates that these locations are very much 'sacred landscapes', and home to fairies and other supernatural beings. For this reason—as well as to avoid the wrath of the otherworldly inhabitants—such sites in Ireland are (even to this day) left well enough alone. Eventually, it was discovered that the Puritan settlers who had acquired the land at Bay soon took to burying what they considered to be a 'devilish' landscape. The local Gaelic Irish community had been driven off the land. The new Puritan owners applied no respect or concern to the curses and superstitions associated with the destruction of these ancient and Pagan 'fairy forts'.

Both the magical operations at house Number 9/9a on Aungier Street, as well as the antiquarian pre-Christian landscape at Bay, had, in each case, been hidden or removed from the intolerant gaze of Puritans in and around the years 1650-60. They are examples of *Folk Magic* cultures and beliefs going back deep into human history and spirituality. Both had gone underground—in more ways than one—and yet, they were rediscovered centuries later and at around the same time. In both cases, the discoveries led to the safeguarding and preservation of these locations for future generations. Sorcery of the past had not only carried the intent of the people responsible for it into the present, but had also preserved the legacy into the future. While the Puritans have long vanished into the course of history, the Pagan and 'devilish' sorcery they had so feverishly sought to exterminate had remained. For all intents and purposes, the spells worked. To quote James Hannam—himself an Oxford and Cambridge PhD—from his excellent book *God's Philosophers*, 'magic works. Sometimes'.

SORCERY'S POETIC UNFOLDMENT

However, this also highlights the natural counter-balance which *Folk Magic* and Pagan mystical beliefs provided against the bigotry and power of the Abrahamic religions—as well as later secular fanatical movements —in that there is always a sense of poetic irony involved. The Puritans of north county Dublin sought to literally seed their own zealotry into the very soil and landscape of the previous stratum which folk magicians and druids had laid down before them. Yet, all the previous magical expression—extending as far back as the proto-shamanism of the Neolithic—had not only remained below their feet, but had eventually erupted to the surface like a volcano of the psyche. A psychic fire of sorcery not necessarily subject to the specific space-time in which these rituals were first performed.

Within the Irish mythological tradition, we can see this use of 'psychic fire'—by means of colorful and simple metaphor—designed so as to burn deeply into the human subconscious mind. In an early translation of the Irish epic, the *Táin Bó Cúailnge*, there is a passage known as *The Intoxication of the Men of Ulster*, in which we are told of an army of war chariots driving with such ferocity across the land of Ulster in the wake of their leader—the teenage hero Cú Chulain—that the 'iron wheels cut the roots of the most immense trees'.

What chance would a 17th century Puritan plowman, muttering a passage from Thomas Watson's *The Godly Man's Picture*, have against an ancient Pagan magical tradition as conveyed within Irish, or any other mythology? Cú Chulain and his fellow warriors unleashing the magical solar fires contained within ancient tree roots—as their chariot wheels cut into them—while they raced towards their adversaries. The description was literally 'charged' with ideas and elements of sorcery and magic. This illustrates the power of sorcery compared to the dogma of religion.

The difference between the syntax, as well as the emotional—if not the inter-generational spoken theatrical resonance—of the *Táin Bó Cúailnge,* told over thousands of years, to that of Thomas Watson's cold examination of the correct observance of the *Sabbath,* demonstrates the power of language itself—as well as that of the spoken word—within the magical tradition. One speaks to the subconscious and remains there for all eternity. The other becomes forgotten within the cognition of a single 'puritanical' existence.

Today—due mainly to the events at Salem, Massachusetts in 1692, the term 'puritanical' has become a byword for everything connected with intolerance and religious mania. As it should. While the 'devilish' crafts which the Puritans sought to annihilate in others have lasted far longer— and are gaining increasing popularity within the consciousness of humans —than that which the fanatical Puritans sought to replace it with. There are now more witches, shamans, druids, warlocks and other practitioners of the magical arts alive today than the sum total of all the Puritans who ever lived, put together.

Something of an unreconstructed indigenous spiritual revival has been taking place since the early 1950s, and is showing no sign of waning. If anything, our advanced technology has only generated more interest in sorcery and the occult. Sorcery is here to stay. Because the sorcery of the past has worked.

PSYCHIC FIRESTORMS

The impetus to write this book came about following a torrent of requests —from people all around the world—in response to a series of Internet videos and radio broadcasts which I had put together on the topic of what magic actually is, and how sorcery actually works. I was pleasantly surprised by the extremely positive response to these broadcasts. Mainly because I had described my personal interest—along with my own unique workings in the world of sorcery and the occult—in very matter-of-fact and direct language. I did not present myself as some great mystic or wizard with any exclusive power or special knowledge. I made no mention of making pacts with angels, cursing my enemies, animal sacrifices, wearing a pointy hat, or any other stereotypical notions concerning the topic. More than anything else, it was that the people who had listened to my talks had responded to tell me that I had made the subjects of magic, sorcery and occult both accessible and human. **This is precisely because magic, sorcery and the occult are accessible and human.** They derived from the folk spirit of our ancestors, and they will always return to that source which is retained deeply within our psyche.

Suddenly, people who had previously found the topic somewhat frightening or complex had lost their sense of overwhelming caution. While others—who found the very idea of something such as sorcery as actually being a real thing to be absurd—appreciated how I had expressed the topic as being interesting, if not intriguing. During these broadcasts—

and likewise, throughout the course of this book—I purposely shied away from (for the most part) availing of archaic esoteric and spiritual language, as well as complex ritualistic theory. Magic ritual is often something we have done all during our lives but have never fully realized what it was we were partaking in.

IN DARKNESS SHINES THE BRIGHTEST LIGHT

A major part of why people were so captivated by my broadcasts was that many had told me that they had listened to them with the lights turned off, and thus, found the experience far more 'intense' than they had expected it to be. Within this darkness, I had boiled the topic down to the meat of the matter. This was due to having spent a lifetime diving into magic, sorcery and the occult at all levels, and from this, I had developed something of a minimalist and bespoke approach to hacking the operating system of the cosmos, which has proven personally fruitful and creatively rewarding for me.

SORCERY'S NEED FOR SECRECY AND SECLUSION

Magic rituals are designed to be very much personal and secretive operations, and are not to be openly broadcast to the world at large. The magic circle has no integrity when this occurs, and the blow-back for both magician and observers—aware that a magical ritual is taking place —can be risky. If not deadly. You build a fortress of conscious *Will*, and you defend it. The *Hedge Schools* of old Ireland were successful because the students were bound to secrecy. This infused the experience with an emotional and psychological charge that further infused the entire experience within a powerful sense of underlying magical vitality. If you plant a fruit orchard, you must protect it, or you will not have a fruit orchard.

More specifically, magical rituals and ceremonies are held in the darkness and seclusion, not because they are evil or sinister, but because our five senses are less subject to exterior sensory distraction when we are surrounded and enclosed by a wall of darkness. Secondary to this is that our senses become extremely heightened within the confines of the darkened space. Removing the totality of full cognitive and sensory awareness from around us, and replacing it with darkness, while also including a single point of light for cognitive focus, such as a fire, or candle flame to target our *Will* upon.

By placing ourselves in near darkness and isolation from public prying, we have far less background noise and unwarranted interruptions to contend with. As a result, there is less 'reality' we need to remove in order to enter into magical states. Our *Will* is more effectively focused— as well as charged—within the full magical experience, while in this situation. We are seeking to incite goosebumps, as well as make the hairs stand on the backs of our necks for reasons we will explore later on in the text. This need for absolute focus is one of the reasons I have always been suspicious of post-*Swinging Sixties* Neo-Pagan rituals involving acts of group nakedness. How can a healthy male—surrounded by attractive naked women—switch off his libido so as to concentrate fully upon the ritual at hand? It is in near total darkness—free from distractions—that we can more easily encounter the other worlds and beings at something of a halfway point.

What worked for our Neolithic and Bronze Age ancestors of the past—entering a central chamber of a passage mound—works equally well today. These tumuli, barrows, cairns and passage mounds were extensions of the rituals of the Neanderthal and Paleolithic cave shamans. This idea then developed to the point where the magic circle—drawn on the floor by the ceremonial magician of the Middle Ages—became a kind of symbolic cave, so as to isolate the focus away from the external world by demarcating it within the confines of the ritual magic circle. We must destroy the conditional reality around ourselves in order to create a psychic vacuum—within our consciousness—whereby other experiences can manifest before us. No one dreams while they are fully awake.

THE MOST ENDURING MAGIC

Folk Magic traditions and practices have stood the test of time because they remain the most honestly integrated forms of occult practice directly connected to who and what we are as humans. From *Voodoo* to *Santeria*, from *Häxan* to *Chaos Magic* (which I consider a technological and culturally expressed form of *Folk Magic*), the 'occult of the people' remains as relevant as ever. It is very much the seed from which all magical and mystical schools and ideas have always germinated. The complex *Alchemy* of the Middle Ages began around an ancient hearth fire, while the ceremonial rites of the *Renaissance* (and later Victorian magical schools) had their origins in the storytelling and simple line drawings of our far-off ancestors. What began as the simplest visual lexicon of magical symbolism—the single point and the line—evolved from being the basic representation of the sperm and egg into a vast and complex collection of magical symbols and designs. Yet all are rooted in the primary conception of the single point and the line. From compass point to circumference into all the geometric symbols we associate with ceremonial and ritual magic today.

Folk Magic is imbued with a natural sense of flux and dynamic alternations, and lends itself well to customization and personalization. Not just across various cultural and racial paradigms, but from individual to individual. Crowley himself pointed this out with his oft-quoted maxim of every man and woman being a star. The reconstruction of our relationships to the cosmos is ultimately a personal experience. No two artists paint the same picture on a canvas identical to one another. No two stars in the cosmos are precisely identical. Reality has a plasticity and malleability that has always been evident to us during the various strange and unusual events which we may have undergone throughout the course of our lives. Even when we didn't see them for what they were at the time of these bewildering experiences.

Yet try to imagine the course of civilization without the impact of magic, sorcery and the occult which is based upon the invocation of such strangeness. It soon becomes apparent that mystical and magical cultures stand equal to—if not more impressive and influential than——secular cultures developed exclusively upon science, economics and/or politics. We are told, for example, that societies which were run upon magical or spiritual ideas tend to be stagnant and backward. Tell this to the people who built the engineering and architectural wonders of ancient Egypt and Sumeria; cultures that were utterly saturated in sorcery and mysticism.

POWERS OF INVISIBILITY

Magical practices are most certainly older than religion and thus, have demonstrated a remarkable tenacity and endurance in the face of on-going persecution. Within the earliest written documents describing the arrival of Christianity in Ireland, reference is made to how Saint Patrick's missionary work was constantly being hampered by druids who used their 'magic' of 'invisibility' to outwit and escape the watchful eye of the invading Roman church. This 'witchcraft' of the druids represented a great challenge for Saint Patrick during his mission to convert the Pagan Irish to the *Church of Rome.* Until, we are told, he himself discovered the sorcery of the druids' 'invisibility' and could then detect their movements and hiding locations. To the modern mind, ideas such as powers of invisibility seem very fanciful—and often completely absurd—until we realize what was meant in those times by 'invisibility'. This was simply referring to camouflage, deception, espionage and deceit. This was the druid's basic form of 'sorcery' when confronted with the Christian threat. This sense of paranoia affected the psychological stability of Saint Patrick, and thus, this imposed sense of insecurity and fear was, in fact, the magical spell itself.

Only until Saint Patrick (or whatever forces that name represented) fully understood this—and then upon utilizing his own 'invisibility'—was he then able to infiltrate the druids of Ireland and rout them out of hiding. However, not completely. Many druids simply pretended to be Christians and instead, entered the church as 'great scholars'. The early *Irish Annals* were using the terminology of the era, of what today we would call this 'invisibility' as being 'the occult': the hidden practices and ideas which can disrupt the reality of a foe, as well as provide protection from being discovered. To torment their minds and lead them into states of confusion and bad judgment. In other words, through mind games and secretive psychological manipulation, the Irish druids were literally able to alter the consciousness of Saint Patrick and that of the early Roman church in Ireland. The frustration—if not paranoia—of Saint Patrick's letters to the Vatican at this time demonstrate how successful the druids' 'invisibility' spell actually was. The secretive and clandestine druids—in the service of the mysterious Cromm Cruach Pagan solar/agricultural tradition—were particularly adept at derailing Saint Patrick's apostolic mission in Ireland.

This deception is still sorcery in the very real sense of the term. When one considers the paranoia and dread that the 'invisibility' of the druids created within the minds of the early Irish Christian missionaries, we can see that this represents a very real shift within the early Christian consciousness. Their ability to function as they wish was always going to be compromised and sabotaged by the druids, who had used their sorcery of stealth and infiltration to gain access into the Roman Church. To the point whereby Saint Patrick was so concerned about the problem that he would only allow priests ordained at Navan Fort to preach the *Gospels*. Saint Patrick—even with the power of the Roman Church behind him— was still bedazzled by the sorcery of the druids. The result being that Christianity took centuries longer to fully establish itself in Ireland than was expected.

WHO IS SPELLBINDING YOU?

This magical deception and altering of consciousness is still very much part and parcel of our everyday lives. By means of the ever-fluctuating miasma of modern perception and awareness, we humans have been carefully cultivated into bio-psychological marionettes suspended inside a sea of state-sanctioned sorcery. Yes, you read that correctly. Real magic and real sorcery, and the ones on the receiving end of this spell craft are

—for the most part—unaware of what is being done to them. The sorcery of today is 'invisible' to most people because they believe that sorcery is something that is only found in the world of make-believe.

ARE MAGIC AND SORCERY EVIL?

Aleister Crowley once famously remarked that *Black Magic* was any kind of sorcery which is not concerned with the mystical self, or personal development. This can be taken as meaning that any form of sorcery which is studied and/or performed to affect or cause change in other individuals—without their granted permission—is *Black Magic*. Although in order to ensure one's survival—while being attacked by others—using magic in this manner is perfectly acceptable. This is an understandable use of *Tactical Sorcery*. The rules of magical engagement are quite clear on this. Do no harm to others, unless they are trying to harm you without good cause.

At the greater level, modern life is filled with assaults upon our consciousness by means of powerful rituals. This could include having your emotions artificially manipulated by an entertainment extravaganza to praying for people without asking them to do this. Good intentions are generally only for the benefit of the 'good', and not for the ones on the receiving end. How many stories have we read concerning charity bosses paying themselves colossal salaries and benefits packages on the back of a photo of a disabled person, or starving Africans. This would be a very common example of *Black Magic* many of us witness in our everyday lives and yet never think of it in such terms.

THE 'CORRECT' KNIFE AND FORK SPELL

When I was growing up, it was considered socially vital to have a complete and total understanding of which cutlery to use at the dining table—when in respectable company—while in a restaurant or at, say, a wedding. Failure to correctly identify, and then use the wrong fork for the wrong course, could result in appalling personal embarrassment and social scandal. As a result, the joy of feasting in the company of others was reduced to a competitive sport based on notions of respectability and social standing.

Yet how many people would have considered this bizarre culinary protocol to be dark sorcery? Indeed it was. The concept was derived from Freemasonic 'great banquets', so that masons could identify one another in social settings depending on how they 'fired their cannons' while out in public. This eventually developed into an overall class-driven neurosis among all respectable diners—fearing they might not be accepted as worthy of such occasions—by using the 'wrong' fork or spoon. I knew people—from when I was a child—who lived in absolute terror of entering a restaurant for fear they might make this fatal mistake. Self-hexing themselves—out of the joy of social feasting—by a simple, but very effective form of dark sorcery.

MAGICAL PROTOCOL

The only magical energy and psychic states we have a right to alter and affect are our own magical energy and psychic states. Yet many people embark upon the path of magical study with the intention of obtaining revenge on another person, or attempting to affect the nature of society—as well as impacting upon the free choices made by the people around them—in order to line their own pockets or exploit them in one way or another. Such approaches to sorcery are what the Victorian occultists decreed to be the work of the *'Brothers of the Left Hand Path'*. What Crowley was essentially—and righteously—telling people to do was to develop yourself spiritually to the point whereby outside 'mystical' (as well as malevolent psychological) forces are no longer capable of causing you problems—within your own life—to the same degree they once did. The occult version of the old paradox of keeping the peace by preparing for war. However, in this case, doing so on a psychic level. Protecting your psychic and spiritual space, so as in order to work—without outside interruptions and stress—towards becoming the best version of yourself you can possibly become.

Our mystical self is just as worthy of understanding and growth as our psychology, intellect and creativity. While there are people who do practice a very deliberate form of deeply narcissistic *Black Magic*, this is, again, giving a false impression of the full experience of developing one's own mystical life. Lack of self-reflection—as well as forgoing

51

continual personal evolution—leads to bad sorcery. Magic must never be used as a crutch, or as an outwardly projecting, compensatory expression of any underlying personal issues—or behavioral faults within your own personality—that you have not properly addressed yourself, first and foremost. You will end up only destroying yourself, and this is indeed evil in the most traditional sense. Evil is 'live' spelled backwards, after all.

LIGHT, SHADE AND CHARISMA

When we ignore the shadow that lurks within us all, we are giving the silent treatment to one half of what we actually are. A painting is made up of light and shadow. This optical illusion brings the painting to life, creating a naturalistic 'punch' to the artwork by accentuating perspective and realism. Our spiritual lives are no different. We need the shadows as well as the highlights—on the canvas of our own spiritual painting—so as to bring our mystical selves to a full and honest potential. This is why we study and practice magic. To generate a greater charismatic charm about us that will bring you more friends than enemies. More help than hindrance. To become a more interesting or attractive painting in the gallery of life. You are not forcing people to gaze upon you. They WANT to gaze in your direction. The term 'charisma' originally meant having the magical power of a god. In fact, all the gods of ancient Greece were considered completely charismatic in the very real meaning of the term. They had the "gift of grace". For a person to have charisma was to have the grace of the gods within one's possession. In the modern sense, this is commonly understood to be someone who has 'it'. This is very different to superficial charm, or creating an artificial persona. Charisma is real and comes from a magical identity emanating from certain individuals.

THE EMERGENCE OF EARTHLY DEMONS

Developing the magical charge within oneself generates a greater personal charisma. In doing this, one is taking a step towards becoming a kind of god. The other side of this coin is the jealousy and envy that will be directed towards you. You will find that these passive dark pawns—consumed by the lack of their own charisma—will emerge from the pathological shadows and into your life as soon as your own charisma develops, and as your magical proficiency increases. This is the price every good sorcerer and sorceress has to pay along the way. Look at this hatred and wickedness of these non-charismatic personalities as the control specimens, allowing you to evaluate your growing magical powers. Remember, magic is a science and an on-going collection of data is vital. These personality types who start attacking you as your charisma generates—and often in the most vicious and surprisingly personal ways—are, in actuality, your lab rats.

This is what makes sorcery so very different to both religion and New Age 'love and light' ideas. An experienced magical practitioner is far better equipped to handle—in a spiritual and psychological sense—the predictable and challenging life experiences and events in which remaining 'unconditionally loving' or 'turning the other cheek' will only result in making you easier meat for what may actually be the predator(s) preying upon you. The object is not to turn the other cheek, but to move the cheek out of the way of the hand about to slap it. So the attacker loses balance and falls over. So as to retain the psychic energy which the attacker was ultimately trying to harvest from you. Anticipate the coming storm surge, then bend like a reed in a torrent, and you'll flourish rather than be washed away.

TRASH MAGIC

Today, sorcery is primarily in the hands of advertising, marketing, public relations, corporations, bureaucrats and also the powerful religions. They spellbind, enchant and charm us constantly, and it is never for our own personal benefit. They generate fears, ignorance, neurosis and insecurities designed to extract all forms of energy from as many people as possible. Personal finances, social status—even the very dynamics of an individual's consciousness—are all meat for the dark corporate and bureaucratic sorcerers who hold sway over their present 'rational' and 'altruistic' chimera, which they constantly lie to us about.

They have set themselves up as something akin to secular gods. Operating between humanity as a whole, and the spiritual destinies they prevent us—as individuals—from exploring for ourselves. Go with the flow, they tell us. As long as it is not your own flow. This is why our world today does not 'feel right' to so many people, and why life itself can seem unsatisfying and empty. That is, if you play the mainstream game according to their rules. Ultimately, it is about a person giving their permission to these powerful magi—and most people willingly go along with the flow—only to find out it was not their flow of energy they followed. It happens via being influenced by—along with attempting to —inadvertently and unconditionally please the *Will* of corporations and cults rather than your own *Will*. Even the most intelligent and aware of us can still so easily become a tumbleweed blowing through the ghost towns of our own making just by following our 'master's' voice. Often, the many people who end up like this only figure out what has been done to them when it is far too late in the game. However, do the same controllers— who forbid us to embark upon our own personal magical and occultic quests—apply the same rules and prohibitions to themselves? Absolutely not. And they never have.

MYSTERY SCHOOLING

Even if you think the very idea of sorcery is pure nonsense and you consider yourself a scientific and rational atheist, I can promise you that just by the mere act of reading this book, you will find the universe and your own life more interesting—as well as becoming a more fuller sensory experience—by the time you are finished. You can close the book after the final page and then consider the text to be 'baloney'. Yet, I can promise you that your subconscious mind will have paid very close attention to the ideas and methods on offer here. You'll find—even if you do not want it—that magical experiences will unfurl within your life. You can call them coincidences, remarkable happenstances or even synchronicity. To be honest, I do not care one way or another if you do consider them 'magical events' or not. Your reaction is irrelevant to the experiences which you will be subjected to. It will still happen, and it will still be sorcery.

Even having written this book—and you reading it—is placing you, the reader, under something of a spell. The ideas and information contained within the pages of this book will find a way deep into your subconscious mind and will remain there for the rest of your life. However, the reader should not concern himself or herself unduly regarding my intentions. Unlike the primary forms of *Trash Magic* sorcery you are currently being bombarded with—getting you to purchase items you don't need, or elect politicians you'll eventually hate—what I am placing into your subconscious is a seed of your own psychic and creative potential. What you do with this information is your own business. Use it wisely, and do no harm to yourself or others who have not harmed you. The universe contains natural laws, and while the cosmos wants you to play with your intentions and dance in tandem with your *Will*, you shall be punished for taking liberties, or unleashing wickedness upon others who did you no intentional harm. For those of you who are more enthusiastically inclined towards the idea of a magical possibility being harnessed within your own lives, I will show you how it is a far easier process than all the complex magical rituals of the past have (somewhat mistakenly) led you to believe. For sorcery, if not anything else, is a product of the level of consciousness which engages with it.

We live in an age where we can send a brief text message to the other side of the world using a small device in the palm of our hand. Depending upon the nature of the message, we can emotionally uplift or destroy the person on the other end receiving the text message. Similarly, sorcery has evolved over time in the same manner. This is not to say the magical and esoteric schools of the past are now obsolete or irrelevant. We are just standing upon the immense foundations they have created for us.

The complex rituals of the Victorian and earlier eras (while often, having great value in their own right) are ostensibly redundant in an age where information is subjected to more and more levels of compression and minimization. The same emotional reactions can be unleashed by someone listening to a *Hip Hop* rap today as would have taken a three-hour-long Wagner operatic production a hundred years ago to generate. We are moving into more simplified—but equally effective—methods of human experience. Sorcery is no less subject to this on-going rationalization of cognition.

FIRSTLY, SACRIFICE YOURSELF

A major component of a magical existence or lifestyle is for people embarking upon this path to cast off the parts of their worldview which can get in the way of individuals fully developing their magical potential. I fully support ideas of honest skepticism and applied caution. However, there are parts of ourselves—which are there as a result of formal education models—that are powerful buffers to our personal magical development. These are traits and habits we need to tame in order for magical forces and the energetic streams of energy—which we require— to pass to and from us. On the other hand, individuals who are overly optimistic about becoming magicians can interrupt the flow of their own energy by being too enthusiastic. In both cases, these issues are ego based.

Measured contemplation and clear focus is how we allow our subconscious minds to communicate and express its wisdom more effectively, so as to better engage the unseen realms with our intention, or *Will*. This must always be a primary consideration. This idea of careful consideration and sacrifice of who we think we are—or, in actuality, who we used to be—is a central idea in many spiritual and magical traditions. Mythology is filled with these tales and parables of sacrifice and self-annihilation, so as to attain new-found wisdom that would otherwise have been impossible to uncover. The *Bull of Minos*—at the center of the labyrinth—will never emerge outside to encounter you.

WHEN ODIN LOOKED WITHIN

Consider the Norse *Eddas* describing Odin and his journey to *Mimir's Well* at the roots of the *Yggdrasil World Tree*. When he arrived at the well, Odin encounters an entity called Mimir, a mysterious being who is aware of all the knowledge of the *Nine Worlds,* which he derives from drinking from the well. When Odin requested to also drink from the well, Mimir refused the god unless Odin sacrificed one of his eyes. Upon gouging out one of his eyeballs, Mimir then dipped his horn into the waters and offered the now one-eyed Odin a draught. Which upon drinking, revealed to Odin the secrets of the *Runes*.

The sacrifice (and risky deal) which Odin made was—in an allegorical context—to allow the subconscious mind to communicate with the mysteries of the cosmos. By removing the entire focus of his cognition away from his worldview. To then allow his missing eye to look *inwards* toward the unseen realms. The deep waters where all the knowledge relating to the dynamics of the cosmos could be attained. In the modern sense, this could be compared to allowing your ego to get out of the way (for a while), and allowing your spiritual potential to come forth. In the case of Odin, his discovery of the secrets of the *Runes* essentially made him a magician.

Odin, who was possibly based on a real Anglo Saxon king of England (Woden/Wotan), must have contained an incredible charisma during his lifetime. So much so, that he was to eventually transform from being a mortal man and into a real god for millions of people across northern Europe and all around the world to this day. In times past, the difference between a man, a king, and a god was the ability to understand and use sorcery in all its forms. This included personal sacrifice. In many ways, the archetype of Odin represents the ideal image of a magician or sorcerer. Although he is a god, he does not behave and act like one. He looks like any other man of a proven vintage. His dress is modest. His power is in his 'invisibility', as he moves through the world of mortal men. For the most part, unnoticed. Taking keen observations of their earthly plight, on his solitary journey between the natural and supernatural worlds. Odin is one of the inspirations for the *Hermit* card in the *Tarot*. Although solitary and inward looking, he carries the eternal power of the cosmos within the glow of the lantern that guides him along his mystical journey.

THE MAGICAL CLASS SYSTEM

On April 2, in the year 999, Sylvester II became the first ever French Pope, and with this, assumed charge of the most powerful political and religious position on Earth. His selection took place at a time before cardinals elected popes. Therefore, his appointment came about as a result of (the then) usual method of power plays between a select number of European noble families at the time. Although there was little debate concerning Sylvester II's qualifications—as he was universally recognized as a great intellectual and teacher—the reason for his selection may have been for reasons far more interesting than his piety or the political and economic opportunities he could offer his sponsors.

Renowned and respected as a brilliant scholar, adept at both Arabic and *Classical* mathematics and astronomy, he had also brought the *abacus* as well as the *armillary sphere*—a complex visual aid designed for instruction in mathematics and astronomy—back into European education and science. Sylvester II is even credited with bringing the decimal number system to the West. As impressive as Sylvester II's *curriculum vitae* was, he possessed another talent which the Vatican (along with his powerful supporters) had hushed up by the time he was on the Papal throne. Pope Sylvester II was once a powerful magician named Gerbert, who had spent many years deeply immersed within the occult world and sorcery of the Iberian and Moorish magical traditions.

Born in 946—in the French town of Belliac—Gerbert soon developed a passion for mathematics and astronomy. He was also fascinated by the Spanish Muslims he witnessed as a boy, as well as taking a deep interest in their customs and traditions. Later, while he was studying astrology in the Islamic-controlled cities of Córdoba and Seville, Gerbert began his career as a sorcerer. This was the result of a magical text—said to have arrived in Spain from the Arab world via an Islamic magi—that came into his possession. When the Arab magician discovered that the future Pope Sylvester II had stolen his book of spells, he went in pursuit of the young Gerbert who—who, much like the druids of Ireland while avoiding Saint Patrick—turned invisible so as not to be located by the incensed Arab. As his study into the occult deepened, Gerbert's reputation as a magician also deepened in tandem with each magical text that came into his possession. A legend soon arose that he had constructed a bronze, mechanical head which contained a female demon by the name of Meridiana, and which could answer questions put to it. The answers were either 'yes' or 'no'. According to later Protestant biographers, it was Gerbert's 'satanic' pact with this demonic female automaton head which allowed him to eventually become Pope. There is probably more than a grain of truth to this.

Soon, things got well out of hand when—legend maintains—Gerbert was killed while at the head of the papal throne, by a demon who was said to have gouged out his eyeballs and dismembered him on the altar. However, the records do not actually specify what kind of 'altar'.

Following his death, a custom eventually took root that the bones inside Gerbert's tomb were capable of afterlife communication by rattling against the sides of his stone coffin. One rattle for 'yes', two rattles for 'no'. Like his demonically controlled bronze robot head, it was something of a binary code of inter-dimensional communication.

MAGICAL SCIENCE

Regardless of the authenticity of some of the more fanciful stories surrounding Gerbert/Sylvester II—which may very well be all true to one degree or another—one thing is certain: during his years of education, he was in the right place, and at the right time, in order to study the magical arts. The theocratic and intellectual frontier between Catholic and Muslim Spain—at that time—was a fluctuating, analog landscape, filled with magicians, alchemists, astrologers and necromancers. It is beyond dispute that the resources and texts necessary for the study of sorcery and the occult were all around Gerbert if he ever wanted access to them.

This was also a time when there was no distinction between sorcery and science. This is not to imply that this was a backward time. Most of the bad press regarding the Middle Ages is due to Protestant historians— much later on in time—fueling the *Reformation* printing presses with anti-Catholic propaganda and rhetoric. Even so, many—if not all—of the great discoveries of the Middle Ages were directly connected to this cross-over period when sorcery and science were one and the same.

Gerbert's seemingly endless desire for knowledge would have been deeply sequestered within the swirling miasma of this occultic environment. Another factor we must take into consideration is that much of the science of the era was a continuation of Pagan sciences, first developed thousands of years prior.

EXCLUSIVE HERESIES

Scientific materialism fails enormously once it is taken out of the self-imposed ghetto of mechanical processes. It cannot adequately explain consciousness, cosmic origins, gravitational effects or, indeed, why approximately ninety five percent of the known universe is currently missing. Science does work very well in explaining and developing mechanistic processes. The solidity of reality is merely an illusion created in our minds. We build matter by observing it. If we can build and construct matter through mere observation, then we can also affect matter with our *Will*. So how can science rationally explain everything, when science is oblivious to most of the universe which has not been resolved into material form by our cognitive awareness?

When scientific materialists think they have found a solution or explanation to something previously considered mysterious, it always leads to more and more complexity—along with further issues—needing to be understood and explained using the same model. From molecules, to atoms, to quarks, strangeness and charm, and on to the 'is it real or is it sorcery' *Higgs Boson*. It just never ends. This is because the next link in the chain is created by observation and study. It is a journey on a road of speculation which, by its very nature, will never end. Not that there is anything wrong with this, per se. The issue that arises is missing out on creating the change within the material universe—by intention—rather than accidental discovery.

Sorcery takes the reverse approach, and instead, compresses complexity into manageable and detectable forces of consciousness and energy directed towards specific goals. The objective is not to measure, quantify, or explain, but to create and generate. The magical process is—for the most part—unconcerned with how the mysterious and unknown phenomena (along with their results) are measured and explained. It is the result itself that matters. As well as knowing how to do it again. The nature and attributes of the unseen forces which created the result are irrelevant, for the most part. Knowing that they exist—without having to perform an autopsy upon them—is enough. The end results are what grant us the gifts of the gods; not developing an obsession with how the gods obtained them to begin with.

After all, this appears to be the primary function of the human brain and nervous system: to limit and compress the entire informational complexity of the universe into a comprehensible and practical model for our personal and collective existence. Without this limiting or compression of everything that ever is, was, and will be—and all of it existing within every part of the universe all at the same time—we would become lost in a maelstrom of infinite possibilities and incomprehensible space-time quantum events and we would, very literally, cease to exist. Considering this, even our nervous system is confining us into the magic circle of our own cognition.

It is by means of this compression and limitation of information that we function as human beings within this five sense reality. However, common experiences of everyday life do sometimes encapsulate the totality of creation in surprising ways. By also accepting and considering the profound nature of such events, we can begin to switch our consciousness into a more magical state of awareness. From that point on, we are not merely observing the game. We are in the game. Odin has gouged out his eyeball.

THE CHARGE

Consider a piece of jewelry—or some other personal object you possess —which has a deeply emotional and/or sentimental value to you. It is not the object itself that contains all the feelings, recollections of experiences and emotions inside it. The object is a means of compressing a myriad of emotions and memories into it. Memories and emotions that are directly connected to our cognition, neurology and bio-chemical neurotransmitters and receptors. It is, rather, the symbiotic associations we have with the object—which we have poured into it—that make it special. This compression—and how it can unleash memories, emotions, as well as very distinct images within our mind's eye, and even changing our heart rate—is what makes the object magical. It is a compression of non-material experiences which we can unleash (very much on demand) by observing, touching or pondering the object.

At the same time, all other sensations and experiences not relevant to the object—and its significance—are, likewise, removed from this experience of sentimental concentration upon the object in order to charge the experiences it unleashes completely into our consciousness. Compression, focus and charge. The experience is one of specific psychic attenuation. As a result of this, it is ultimately one of personal amplification of its significance and meaning.

Science, on the other hand, explores the component nature of such an experience without giving credence to the overall experience itself. It dissects it into, quite literally, oblivion. What starts out as an examination of the properties of the object—along with the biochemistry connected to any emotional responses it may generate—ultimately breaks down into a dissolution of ever-widening mechanistic criteria. In the end, the overall experience is lost. Eventually, this exploration into smaller and smaller components leads to nowhere and nothing. The hugeness of the CERN *Hadron Collider*—along with all the infrastructure and human intellect involved in its construction and operational complexity—is directed towards the ultimate nothingness of things. The same nowhere and nothing which science tells us created the *Big Bang*. To the magician, it does not really matter how the universe came into existence. The important thing is that the universe exists, and we are part of it.

SORCERY TO SUPPLEMENT SCIENCE

By pointing this out, I am not bashing science, nor am I promoting religion. Science has improved our lives greatly in terms of health and living standards. Even so, scientific materialism knows very, very little in real terms. They are not "almost there" in explaining everything as they have constantly proclaimed in recent decades. This stance is no different from the same faults they point out in religious fanatics, and is more akin to a delusional psychosis meets narcissism meets dogma. How can they make outrageous statements such as, "we are very close to figuring it all out", when they can only locate five percent of the universe around them to begin with? The fact is that when they are confronted with such issues, the vanguards of scientism behave very much like the intolerant religious zealots they claim to be so against. There is no difference between smugly stating, 'we are working on finding these things out', and a bishop in the Middle Ages invoking 'sacred mysteries'. As Aleister Crowley himself pointed out in this regard, "Science is always discovering odd scraps of magical wisdom and making a tremendous fuss about its cleverness."

Unfortunately, scientific materialistic limitations are then passed onto society as a whole. I believe this has handicapped most humans in terms of allowing them to reach their own personal full potential in life. As a result, they write off incredible experiences as 'coincidence' because there is no way to scientifically explain how these 'strange experiences' occurred and why. So, rather than marveling and enjoying these experiences for what they are—as well as exploring what they represent so as to determine if they can lead to further remarkable experiences—they simply just ignore them. We do not need to believe in magic, gods and supernatural experiences, as such. However, by acknowledging these experiences for what they are, our lives can become ultimately more satisfying and creative. By honoring their symbols and archetypes as representative of forces of nature in tandem with the dynamics of the psyche.

What we do know is that the scientific method has been successfully used to quantify results and experiments which demonstrate that human consciousness and thoughts do affect the very nature of reality. Time and time again, these ideas of 'mind over matter' have been proven to exist. The problem which then arises is that science refuses to accept the results because they can't verify every stage of the process, nor repeat the experiments with identical findings. Sorcery is an art; it will never produce the same two or fifty results precisely. Approximately ninety five percent of the universe is neither detectable nor measurable. This unseen realm of the unknowable is the domain from which all magical experiences both arise from and are connected to. Only the observable effects within this reality are self-evident. This ability to see and observe the effects of unknown forces is what makes them real; not the ability to explain or accurately measure them.

TERMS AND CONDITIONAL THINKING

Terms such as sorcery, magic, witchcraft, hexing and so on, are words which have been universally handicapped solely by the images which they conjure up among the mass of society. In that, within our modern world, most people are conditioned to automatically ridicule, or be amused by/fearful upon hearing them. We are told—as soon as we exit our childhood—that such things belong to the far-off ignorance-bounded miasma of ancient history. Or else, they are retained—during the present era—only within the logical fallacies of the misguided and deluded. Is this a rational and reasonable assumption which most people are making in reaction to the very mention of terms associated with the study and practice of occultism and ritual magical process? Are these people being honest with themselves and those of us who seek answers beyond the material realms?

Many thousands of scientists have been, and still are, members of esoteric organizations such as Freemasonry and so on. Yet, aside from these fraternal associations—along with any the ritualistic and ceremonial aspects they are connected to—a surprisingly large number of the most famous and respected scientists throughout history were also ardent sorcerers. They did not simply 'dabble' in the occult; they were serious magicians. Sir Isaac Newton, for example, made absolutely no distinction between his hard scientific work and his pursuit of sorcery. From the French astronomer Camille Flammarion to the legendary 'rocket-fueled anti-Christ' Jack Parsons himself, the list of 'serious' scientists who were also magicians is literally too numerous to mention.

So the question must then be asked: why, in a world where we are told magic does not exist—and that only science can unlock the secrets of the universe—is it that time and time again we see this rule being violated by the ones who create and uphold it? The answer is that there is something within magic and sorcery which they find useful and accessible to some degree. Yet, like the global financial system, the world of magic and sorcery contains its *haves* and *have nots*.

THE SHADOW CRAFT

There is most certainly a magical class system in effect, and what we are told is pure nonsense, is—when one scratches the surface—taken very seriously by the elite strata of Western society. For all their 'rational' grandstanding, not much has changed from the time when kings held court alongside druids, wizards and magicians. Within this magical exclusiveness, and the clandestine use of magic by elite structures—in the past, and also into the present—is a very useful observation we can make for ourselves.

The elites keep their magical intention and *Will* secret. They do not broadcast their *Will* and desires to the world, and neither should any prospective magician reading this book. Is this exclusively done so as to rule us as their ignorant sheep? Not entirely. The lesson we are being shown here is the 'Dark Arts' really are just that. Magic rituals and practice must be done in secret and out of the sight of others. This is why they have all the power. This is the means whereby some of us are going to take back our own power.

The compression of experience into a confined space of purposeful deprivation away from the 'real world' and its many stimuli is the foundation of successful magical practice. The wizard works in his lonely tower for a reason. The fact that this magical isolation has been in effect for thousands of years—as a central idea of ritual sorcery—gives testament to its value. Any prospective magician should take heed and make sure to safeguard their sacred space. Even if a coven is performing a magical ritual with several members, secrecy is key to the success. This psychic isolation can—and should be—cultivated on an individual level by long walks alone in the woods. Preferably at night, and as long as there are no predators present. Find ways to be alone, isolated and deprived of as much artificial environmental background noise and distraction as possible, so as to embrace the liberating darkness of solitude. Like the *Hermit* card in the *Tarot*, the more you wander in the darkness, the brighter your lamp will glow so as to guide you towards your desires.

STOLEN SORCERY AMONG THE GREAT AND GOOD

In June 1991, a conference was held at Fordham University in New York entitled *The Occult and Modern Soviet Russian Culture,* and which was sponsored by none other than the highly influential *Soros Foundation.* Along with several other well-respected endowments and research councils, who all gave their enthusiastic blessing to this event, an academic study into the practice of sorcery and the occult within the Soviet Union. Paid for, and attended by, some of the most powerful individuals and groups in the world. The list of professors and influential figures who attended this conference—where the 'magical booty' from the Soviet Union was first presented—would have been enough to wipe the smirk off the face of the average self-professed debunker.

Ask yourself why—practically as soon as the *Iron Curtain* and Soviet Union fell—did scores of Western academics, representing some of the most esteemed universities in North America and from around the world embark on something akin to an occultic fire sale in order to get their hands on as many books, documents, and especially, the findings of scientific research programs dealing with the occult and sorcery during the heyday of the Soviet Union, if indeed, all this stuff is just nonsense? We are not merely talking about an antiquarian expedition to locate some lost books of European and Asiatic esoteric history.

This was the very specific procuring of documentation and research papers into Soviet occultic sciences and practices, within a recently fallen super power during the scientifically-minded 20th century. Why was so much time, academic resources and serious money put into collecting the 'woo' of the commies? The answer is because academia, powerful bodies and certain institutions wanted to get their hands on this magical research and keep it exclusively for themselves alone. Just as they have done so since the time of the *Enlightenment*.

Not only this, but the texts and research pertaining to the occultic legacy of the Soviet Union were eventually placed under the jurisdiction of the *Library of Congress.* Alongside—just by sheer chance—the occult and esoteric documents and files of Adolf Hitler and the *Third Reich.* Which were captured by the US Army during the final weeks of the *Second World War*. If, indeed, none of this stuff was in any way real—or at any level worthy of study and examination—then why bother collecting and archiving it with the same level of importance that was given to German rocketry development or Soviet submarine design? People you know—in your everyday life—may scoff at the idea of sorcery, and that of magical forces and consider the concept to be absurd and laughable. However, the people who control your thoughts and culture—and that of the intellectual and political destiny of this planet—take sorcery and the occult very seriously. They always have done so. This is the same reason why Roman generals took time to study the sorcery of the druids of Gaul and how they influenced their own 'barbaric' society. While today, those who control the constantly meandering spectrum of what you think are your own personal opinions, give you the high priests of reductionist dogma in the form of Richard Dawkins, Brian Cox and Bill Nye. In order to make you feel brilliant, clever and reasoned, and all this while the powerful captains of modern society and popular culture are attending academic conferences dealing with the occult and sorcery.

While you're watching some *National Geographic* TV documentary bluffing you into thinking that the great stone monuments of the ancient world were created by superstitious ape-like simpletons with deer antler picks and reed ropes, the men and women of state-sanctioned scientific and political common sense are busying themselves with the complexity of ancient grimoires, along with the study of occultic and supernatural forces within and outside the human body. They are especially fascinated with ideas concerned with the projection of mental thoughts beyond the human brain. Why wouldn't they be—considering who and what they are —when you think about it? Always finding ways to make the magical arts work for their own power and agendas, their efforts have borne fruit.

All you have to do is look at who has the power and influence in our world today.

THE EXCLUSIVE MAGICAL HOARDS OF THE ELITE

In response to this revelation surrounding the nature and objectives of the 1991 Fordham conference, the average person would simply respond by claiming that the academic collection and study of Soviet occultic literature and research materials was merely acquired as a part of the overall historic record. An insight into the sociology of the USSR. Or perhaps, something to point to as proof of the Soviets being both lost as a political administration, and as an expression of their failed political idealism.

If this be the case, then how does this explain why the atheistic and scientifically-minded Soviet leadership supported the work of occult artists such as V.N. Chekrygin? An artist whose paintings dealt with the idea of the Soviet sciences using space travel and cosmology in the pursuit of what was termed 'extra-ecclesiastical activity'? That being, using Soviet spacecraft and radio telescope technologies to resurrect dead ancestors on this earth, as well as on other planets? In other words, something akin to a kind of Marxist Cosmological Necromancy. This idea even spilled over into Soviet cinema with the highly acclaimed 1972 movie *Solaris,* which was based on the 1961 novel of the same title by Stanisław Lem. The story deals with humanity's 'anthropomorphic limitations' while attempting communication with extraterrestrials. A rather uneconomical method of describing demonology. Once more, we are dealing with a purposely self-conscious anti-spiritual worldview that was still availing of spiritual and magical ideas during a futile attempt to avoid its own impending irrelevancy.

The Soviet leadership was indulging in these supernatural and mystical concepts for the same reason that Cornelius Vanderbilt put all of his financial speculation into the hands of a stage actress and mystic named

Victoria Woodhull: because sorcery does work and people of power do understand that the material world is affected—and dependent upon—non-material forces of the cosmos. Forces which are profoundly connected to human consciousness and desires. To cite J.P. Morgan when he remarked, "Millionaires don't use *Astrology*, billionaires do." Stated, no doubt, during an off-guard moment. When the rest of us were given an insight into how the rich and powerful live by their own magical codes while they tell the great unwashed that it is nonsense.

Sorcery does produce results, and these results are both self-evident and verifiable if you bother to examine the history of the occult. Consider the many scientific research programs which have seriously studied and evaluated magical and other unknown supernatural phenomenon and forces, and to a far greater degree than is generally known by the average man or woman in the street. Every major university and institution of learning has conducted numerous investigations into the occult for as long as these institutions have been in existence. This situation still continues to the present day. What took place at Fordham in 1991 was hardly unique.

PETER THE GREAT'S STATE SORCERER

The use of sorcery in the affairs of the Russian state was not just limited to the Soviet Union by any means. General James Bruce (1669-1735)—

or 'Count Jacob' as he was commonly known—was the *Scientific Advisor* to Peter the Great. Irrespective of this grand title, his position was more akin to that of a royal wizard. He was also Russia's first royal astronomer, and one of the powerful individuals behind the design and construction of Russia's first large scientific telescope, which was housed within the top floor of the *Sukharev Tower* in Moscow.

Of Scottish noble descent, Bruce's personal book and manuscript collection formed a substantial part of what eventually became the *Russian Academy of Sciences'* library. The majority of these texts were occultic and *Alchemical* in nature. His observatory allegedly also contained some of the most forbidden books devoted to the study and practice of dark magic, which were rumored to have been walled up inside the *Sukharev Tower* before his death. The *Sukharev Tower* also housed the *Moscow School of Mathematics and Navigation*. Time and time again we see this link—from John Dee in the Elizabethan court to the influence of the Templars/Freemasonry during the great Portuguese *Age of Discovery*—between royal occultism, navigation and seafaring.

Count Jacob's main function was to create a magical almanac known as the *Black Book,* using a system of divination referred to as the 'water of life', which would cause demons to appear and offer their services— generally in regards to revealing future events—to the leaders of the Russian state, or anyone else who possessed Count Jacob's almanac. The *Black Book* remained in print until 1912. Incidentally, this was the same year that Rasputin ostensibly became the state mystic of Imperial Russia, due to his influence over the Czarina Alexandria. The *Sukharev Tower* itself was looted and finally demolished by the Soviet government in 1934. No records exist as to what happened to the purported vast library of *'Black Magic'* texts rumored to have been held there. We can only assume that if the Soviets found them, they must have held on to them. Atheism for the masses, sorcery and occultism for the powerful elite, regardless of any prevailing political or theocratic associations currently in vogue.

THE CURSE OF CHERNOBYL

Being something of a capitalistic magician, Cornelius Vanderbilt became incredibly wealthy by employing the magical services of the 'magnetic healer' and spiritualist Victoria Woodhull. Who, incidentally, was also the first woman to run for *President of the United States*. This is akin to mystic capitalism. On the other hand, within the official godless world of international communism, the Soviet state mystics realized they were doomed—as an idealistic society—when on April 26, 1986, the *Number 4 Reactor* at the *Chernobyl Nuclear Power Plant* ruptured, and became a catastrophic nuclear disaster. Soon it was recognized that the reactor had been 'cursed' from the start. When the Soviet leadership lost control of the situation, sorcery invariably took over. The term 'Chernobyl'—within Slavic witchcraft—just so happens to be the Russian version of the incantation *'Abracadabra'*. It is said that prayer is usually the last refuge of a scoundrel. If the scoundrel happens to be a powerful individual or institution, then it is sorcery which becomes their last refuge. The power plant itself was built within the heart of a Ukrainian 'magical' landscape steeped in Slavic occult and folklore traditions. At first, the Soviet leadership kept the disaster quiet, but when the full implications of the disaster became apparent, coupled with their sense of dread and doom at the realization of the curse having been unleashed, the Russian news agency, TAS, waited until April 30, or the 'witches sabbath' of *Walpurgis Night,* to break the news of the disaster to the world.

If this wasn't remarkable enough, within the Ukrainian language, the word "Chernobyl" also translates as the name for the toxic plant known as Wormwood. Within Hebrew mysticism, the term for Wormwood translates as *'la'anah'.* Which means "curse" in both Arabic and Hebrew. *La'anah* even makes its way into the *Book of Revelations,* which is the only magically-orientated book of the Christian Bible. Being essentially a complex curse issued against the Roman Emperor Nero, "The third angel sounded his trumpet, and a great star, blazing like a torch, fell from the sky on a third of the rivers and on the springs of water. The name of the star is Wormwood. A third of the waters turned bitter, and many people died from the waters that had become bitter."

The 1991 conference at Fordham University, funded by the likes of George Soros—and attended by some of the top academics of the time— came into being for no other reason than these Western academics and globalists are just as amazed and fascinated by the strangeness of such phenomenon as the Chernobyl/Wormwood revelation as much as you are (probably) reading about this right now. The unfolding mythological aspects, as well as the synchronistic occurrences surrounding the emerging 'sorcery' of the likes of the Chernobyl disaster, would have been duly noted by the Western elites.

Our rational and scientific overlords are fully aware that there are forces beyond the material world which are profoundly interconnected with human consciousness. That these supernatural events and experiences do in fact exist. How these forces can be called upon—directly, or else become unleashed through 'curses'—and can also be used to affect changes within this material reality. Not to mention, as predicting, if not influencing the outcome of future events. At some point, the notions of coincidence and chance have to step to one side, as other, less prosaic assumptions demand to be entertained. Naturally, they will never admit such things as a profound interest—let alone, their well-documented beliefs and practice—into sorcery and the occult, publicly.

A lot of this has to do with the fact that they can't measure nor accurately reproduce these bewildering phenomena using the accepted scientific methods. They are put at something of a useful disadvantage by the demands of their own ethos. In that, what they can't fully understand themselves puts them under no obligation to explain such experiences to the rest of us. Denial of the craft has been standard practice since the formation of Freemasonry. Along with the cover story being put out there that ceremonial rituals of these occult societies are merely a social aspect of the craft, partaken for fraternal and traditional pursuits, and enacted by reasoned, respectable and rational gentlemen.

These are the same reasoned, respectable and rational American billionaire industrialist gentlemen who hired 'magnetic healers' as personal magicians. The same reasoned, respectable and rational gentlemen who took the *Spiritualism* movement of the late Victorian era very seriously. Even into the domain of the sciences and emerging technologies of the period. The same reasoned, respectable and rational gentlemen who then filled magical orders such as the *Ordo Hermeticus Aurorae Aureae.* Otherwise known as *The Hermetic Order of the Golden Dawn.* The same leaders of society who tell you to laugh and scoff at the occult and magical ritual, while they themselves take it very seriously. The class system didn't begin and end with economics alone.

Their gated communities protect much more than the family jewels and silver cutlery from the hands of the 'unclean' and 'profane'.

AS ABOVE, SO BELOW

We—all of us—are forces which represent the untapped potential of sorcery and the occult. Located within, and deriving from the lower poles of our consciousness, it is a part of us as much as the biological processes within our bodies. Our very life force comes complete with a star of magical potential which sparkles from inside us. Like the ancient megalithic builders of the past, this star within us can be aligned and called upon to shine its light towards illuminating locations and ideas we have created and set into conjunction with its presence.

Firstly, we have to be aware of its existence by removing the clouds of social conditioning and modern life, which hides it from our earthly gaze. The greatest revelation which I have uncovered from a lifetime of study of sorcery and occult sciences is that we all have this shining star of magical potential contained within us, and this inner power is waiting to be tapped into and be allowed to burn as brightly as possible.

HOW TO MAKE REALITY MALLEABLE

We are all capable of altering the material world—to some degree or other—by following specific steps and processes. Some are better than others at achieving this. However, we can all attain surprising results if we put a saddle on the devil's back and ride him towards a better neighborhood inside this present purgatory of human existence which we currently reside within. Feeling a bit put off by the 'saddle on the back of the devil' metaphor? No worries. Let's pretend he is a bicycle instead, although I am still partial to the devil analogy. As in the esoteric sense, the devil is simply an archetype representing powerful primal forces. However, I also understand that the scary guy with the horns and tail still has a lot of bad press to contend with. So we'll stick with the bicycle metaphor.

Sorcery is no more unattainable to the average lay person than learning to ride a bicycle. In fact, learning to ride a bicycle is a perfect analogy for one's own personal engagement with sorcery and occult forces. As with any two-wheeled bicycle, we first have to understand its mechanical processes and what it can offer us. How the wheels turn in synchronization with our feet moving the pedals. How the direction of travel is controlled by the turning of the handlebars. The potential dangers of not keeping our feet on the ground when we stop moving. The vital necessity of using the brakes while being aware of our current location, as well as any potential dangers we may encounter while operating the bicycle while it is in motion. There is a learning process. This is how evolution works, and all forms of energy are not free. We must engage with the process.

The practice of magic and sorcery functions in just the same manner as mastering the use of a bicycle, in that it is not a free ride. We fall. We can get hurt. We get up and try again. However, by means of this trial-and-error process towards the proficient operation of the pedals and handlebars—in conjunction with how we balance our body and focus our mind—we begin to continually refine the skill. Primarily via our subconscious, background processes, so as to develop a surprisingly powerful relationship with the mechanical nature of the bicycle, along with its relationship to the environment we are traveling within. As we master this, we are then able to move further along the road.

We soon become better at it. In time, it is second nature—the 'art' has taken over—and all the fears and trepidation concerning our vulnerability while sitting on the saddle and cycling have been overcome. The idea of this 'second nature', of our subconscious taking over new tasks and abilities, was termed *The Robot* by the British author Colin Wilson. It is representative of the latent power within all humans to reach beyond the present limitations of ourselves as individuals, and as a species. Learning the art of sorcery and the craft of magic works in precisely the same way. In fact, for all intents and purposes, the mastering of learning to ride a bicycle is an act of sorcery in and of itself, in that the rider has called upon previously unknown forces—*The Robot,* or whatever term one wishes to use—contained within himself or herself so as to create a new experience within this material, five-sense reality. That experience being that he or she ie now a cyclist. Something he or she never was before. Partaking of an experience that previously never existed for us—and more significantly, for the world around us—within this reality model. Our internal, personal shift in consciousness, has, likewise, become *novelty* within the wider world, and the overall reality model of the universe has become slightly more complex.

We are all—regardless of whether we understand it or not—building the universe every day of our lives. This is the passive sorcery we partake in constantly, unaware of what we are actually doing. Tactical, rather than passive sorcery, represents the objectives to do it with focused intention and *Will,* towards specific outcomes, to transcend the mortal, passive observer and attain godhood. Following our mastery of the bicycle (assuming we are still alive), we then become aware of the new-found possibilities that our physiology—in tandem with this mechanical contraption—can provide us with. We can now go places, improve, and greatly expand our overall experience of life while improving our health. Discover new locations and sights we never knew previously existed. Unfold very personal revelations about ourselves we never knew were present within us. Amazing events and surprises then happen. We may not have discovered the love of our life, or began to take an interest in a specific aspect of the natural world, had we not learned to ride a bicycle. Or before we took that turn down a quiet country lane—for reasons we don't recall—only to meet a beautiful woman we fell in love with. Or to behold a landscape for the first time, which left a deep and lasting impression upon us. You see where I am going with this?

MAGICAL LIMITATIONS

However, along with this new world of experience and possibilities, we also uncover our own potential insofar as to what they can provide us with. This is the most important lesson of all for any prospective magician. **Sorcery is an art that some of us are better at than others.** Not all of us can win the *Tour De France* just because we can now ride a bike. This is due to our proficiency at being a cyclist is limited by who and what we are at the time in our lives, as well as our location in the world and the specific society in which we live. We can't pedal a bicycle to the moon, no matter how proficient we become.

Sorcery is subject to similar limitations. Our own personal limitations. The baseline from which you start upon your magical and occultic path is the starting location that determines how far you can go. Born in an inner-city ghetto, you can get out of the slum and improve your life no end comparatively to how you started out in life. Born wealthy, you can use sorcery to allow you to appreciate your good fortune in winning the lottery of life, then use it for the betterment of humanity and the world in general. Assuming, that is, you are not a class-obsessed aristocrat with a megalomaniacal, self-ordained destiny to control the existence of the human race as if they are your pets. See the Fordham University conference if you still need reminding that this kind of thing actually goes on. Magic and occult practice are now well within the grasp of a large proportion of the human race—than had been generally available in Western terms—since the Middle Ages, when the social order of things became far more complex and centralized. However, it is vital that we keep our emerging magical talents as secretive as possible.

PERSECUTION OF WITCHES

The prohibition and ruthless extermination of anything connected to witchcraft and sorcery came about as a result of an increasingly powerful elite group—mandated by the *Church of Rome*—and who felt threatened by the *Folk Magic* of the times, along with other types of witchcraft and surviving paganism, which was also very much part of everyday life in both urban and rural poor communities of the period. *Folk Magic* and its 'witches' were subsequently brutally suppressed, and from this, the rise of the elite esoteric occult and magical orders then began in earnest. Securing the authority of the emerging medical and legal professions, academia—as well as the Abrahamic religions—also played a huge part in these witch hunts. The primary reason for the suppression of sorcery and witchcraft was to wipe it out among the masses. In other words, the ruling elite took what was central to all human cultures, then kept it for themselves alone. Once the age of witch burning and persecutions were completed, ridicule and mockery replaced the *breaking wheel* and the *thumbscrew*.

Until recent times, this has remained the case. The upper echelons of society—from the major religions to the aristocratic classes—have used the education system to 'reason' the supernatural out of us, while they themselves still continue to study and practice sorcery before our very eyes. Everything, after all, comes down to energy. Money, food, fuel, sex, political and corporate power. Therefore, sorcery and the occult sciences are energy manipulation and control methods which the wealthy and powerful have kept from the rest of us. Just as they have with their crown jewels and their vast tracts of private lands.

FROM RITUALS TO ENTERTAINMENT

There is no difference between the opening and closing ceremonies of the *Olympic Games*, *World Cup Finals* or the *Superbowl*, and that of the sorcery and occult rituals which took place at Stonehenge, Delphi or Karnak in ancient times. The only difference is that the shamans, druids or priests of the past were honest and upfront with the population in telling them that they were performing rituals. While today, we are told it is just 'entertainment'. Then we somehow feel compelled to purchase a brand of diet soft drink we had previously not desired... While the magic of the agrarian cultures never fully went away, it has officially evolved into 'customs' and 'superstitions'. Today, with the advent of the Internet, it has become resurgent once more, albeit in a less localized form. Spooling itself from out of the electromagnetic spectrum and into the consciousness of a new generation of healers, wise women, druids and herbalists. Websites and endless on-line articles have opened up a whole new world of delicious heresies for those seeking to find them. We no longer need to acquire a vast personal library of books on sorcery and the occult in our homes, although it is vital to own, and read, at least some paper and bound magical texts, for there is an important spiritual experience in the very act of doing so.

More people than ever are taking part in the greatest occult revival since the final remnants of the *English Witchcraft Laws* were abolished in 1951. The implications of this are enormous. Although this book is aimed at the solo practitioner, I would not discourage people (if they wish to do so) from joining ceremonial magical circles and groups. Apart from the social aspects, there are helping hands and often valuable guidance to be found within them. Ultimately, you are seeking to generate a greater charge emanating from the star within yourself. If this arises by means of joining a *Wicca*, *Golden Dawn*, *OTO* or any other group—and then partaking in their respective rituals and studies—then by all means, do so. This is your experience. Some people prefer their star to hang by itself in the cosmos, while others enjoy the sympathetic beauty of forming a constellation. It's your call. I would suggest, though, that people read this book to its completion before making any decisions one way or the other. By the time you are done with the text, you'll know your own magical self—as well as the purposeful magical experiences that have been imposed upon your life—much better. Even experiences which you now take for granted—such as your perception of the passing of time—will take on a whole new understanding and awareness.

ARBITRARY SPACE-TIME AND THE ARRIVAL OF LOKI

Consider how your mind processes time depending on the situations you are experiencing at certain moments. When you are bored or nervously waiting for the results of something important to arrive, time drags into a seemingly endless and torturous experience. By contrast, consider how time flies while enjoying a vacation or being at a rock concert. The perception of the space-time experience is completely subjective to the consciousness of the individual who is experiencing it. Your mind speeds up or slows down according to external sensory factors. It's an extremely personal sensation of perception.

A person sitting next to you on the train could be experiencing the unfolding of space-time within their own conscious mind to a completely different degree than what you may be experiencing on the same train, on the same track, going in the same direction, and at the same speed. Now let's apply this experience to you—as a magician—generating this same effect within another person, by making them wait in anticipation for something they strongly desire. Then, delivering what they desire and immediately causing the clock-speed of their brains to rapidly increase, in accordance with how you have actually altered their own perception of space-time awareness and experiences. Initially, by first withholding from them what they wanted. Then finally delivering to them what they wanted. Now that is the power of magic.

Understanding this phenomenon within a magical framework, your memories of your childhood Christmas Eve insomnia—followed by running downstairs to open your presents in the morning—take on a whole new meaning when you apply a magical narrative to the experience. Time had no meaning relating to the clock on the wall as you lay in bed all night long anticipating what was inside the packages with your name on them below the Christmas tree. Likewise, you had no memory of running down the stairs so you could open your presents with great excitement. Then, before you knew it, it was lunchtime.

It was all 'inside your own head', and your perception of space-time was being altered by external events, which meant nothing in terms of the clock on the wall. This is before we even apply how these childhood Christmas memories—in terms of emotions and symbols—burn deeply into your subconscious, and remain there for the rest of your life. It's also worth pointing out that pine trees, *yule logs*, the star on top of the tree, and even Santa himself (Odin) are all based on Pagan magical customs. Old sorcery never fades away. It merely becomes re-branded. This is but a simple demonstration of sorcery and how it can be used to alter the reality of yourself, or someone else. From the long endless pauses taken by Adolf Hitler before addressing the Nuremberg mass rallies, to the last five minutes of a soccer game in which your team is winning and every single second appearing to take longer than all the previous ninety minutes of play, to the moments before the birth of your child, seemingly lasting longer than the first few years of their lives. These are all—in one way or another—very real magical experiences. The rules of 'normal' space-time were altered.

A watched kettle never boils for the same reasons. In that, we are placing our concentration into a process which—for the most part—is outside of our personal control. A process that began when the turbines—belonging to the electrical utility provider—started generating electrical current. In other words, waiting for the kettle to boil is (indirectly) teaching you a valuable lesson about the magical space-time process. You were not there at the start of the process, so you can't control the outcome, apart from switching off the kettle. Your torturous anticipation is the reveal of your own overall detachment—or lack thereof—from the entire process. You are sacrificing yourself to the utility company, so as to gain a small piece of the greater powers of the utility company. Not that there is anything wrong with this, as such. However, it is a sacrifice which can teach you a lot about yourself if you consider it in a magical light. Remember what I wrote previously in the text; about how once we step onto the magical path, nothing is ever 'ordinary' again?

Your subconscious mind knows that you did not generate the electricity to boil the water inside the kettle, so it slows down space-time in order to teach you something about your own lack of engagement with the overall process. It takes seemingly forever because you have no control over the full dynamics of the situation. The real magician, in this case, is the electric company who changed steam, rushing water, wind or sunlight into flowing electrons of pure current, which have then passed through your electrical meter and into your kettle or electric stove.

You are not controlling the game; you are just a part of it. The end outcome is the electrical utility company getting you to pay for the 'charge'. Your subconscious mind is letting you know this with each torturous second you are waiting for the kettle to boil. The subconscious mind never lies. It is the greatest teacher and mentor of any magician or witch. You pay attention to how it alters your own perception of space-time. In this case, being informed (intuitively) of a wasted 'charge' you need for something else **which you can implement and control**. Sorcery is an art unsuited to those seeking instant, immediate gratification and outcomes. It is, rather, an art suited to those who cherish and work with their own intuitive insights. The Ancient Greek philosophers termed this as being 'noetic', and was also considered to be the supreme doctrine of the *Divine Intellect*. Herein lies the greatest misunderstanding of sorcery: that we can implement change within the material universe instantly.

Nothing in the cosmos ever happens in an instant. Even a flash of lightning represents the end result of geothermal and electrical processes which have taken a certain time period—and under very specific circumstances—to develop in the atmosphere over the course of the storm's life-cycle. The process is neither automatic or precisely measurable. The discharge of electricity—which may have begun as a pure stream of energy—eventually manifests into a dispersed fork of lightning discharging downwards. Although this hits the target which drew its attention, it may also produce a surprising and unexpected outcome. It is, after all, a fork of lightning, and not a spear of lightning.

THE ARRIVAL OF LOKI

Mjölnir—the hammer of Thor—still had to be forged from raw materials within the workshop of the dwarven magicians Eitri and Brokkr. The finalization of any magical event presents the collective outcome over time. The unfolding of the craft, spell or conjuration is often surprising, poetic and even ironic. As Thor found out when Loki—having transformed into a horse fly—bites the dwarf magician Brokkr on the eyelid and makes him lose concentration at a vital moment, thus causing Thor's hammer to have a shorter handle than was intended. When working with sorcery, prepare to encounter Loki in many guises and outcomes. Patience is vital, along with adaptability to unexpected happenstance during the course of the magical process. This is what makes the difference between an apprentice and a master.

THE MYSTERIOUS FAIL SAFE AND NECESSARY DAEMON

One of the most enduring mysteries of sorcery—and one I have personally pondered for many years—is the remarkable dynamic background processes which the magical system implements so as to impose certain limitations (as well as enlightening lessons and personal revelations) upon the magician or witch. It is almost as if the very act of magical awareness and practice itself generates a temporary supplemental consciousness of its own. One that exists throughout the entire magical process. The *daemon* of the Ancient Greeks was the supernatural expression of the moral imperative, and the muse of the painter and poet.

Call it what you want, but it readily becomes manifest as soon as we begin the magical process. Aleister Crowley initially outlined that "magic is the Science and Art of causing change to occur in conformity with *Will*." Yet this *Will* is not an inert operation entirely under the absolute assiduity of the magician or artist.

THE MUSE OF CONJURATION

It could be argued, for example, that the character of Stephen in James Joyce's novel *Ulysses* was conjured up by the novel's hero Leopold Bloom during his one day of walking the streets of Dublin in 1904. When Bloom spends the day moving from the basic, daily—ego and biological survival and reward—processes of his cognition, he slowly migrates his conscious focus towards the absolution and personal redemption of his own neurosis. Bloom's passive conjuration takes place during an early Summer's day filled with all his personal epics, trials, torments, perversions and fantasies. As a result of his intense awareness—regarding the strangeness of his life—being a Jew in early 20th century urban Ireland. Within the novel, Bloom slowly manifests Stephen as the compensatory *Daemon* of his dead son Rudy in order to resolve his broken relationship with his promiscuous and adulterous wife Molly, who is the unresolved tragic epicenter of all his emotional and psychological issues. But Bloom could not do it alone. He needed a *Daemon*, and so he subconsciously manifested Stephen for this purpose. The character of Molly Bloom is something of an artistic conjuration of James Joyce's intense relationship with his own real-life wife Nora Barnacle, who was a formidable woman in her own right, and something of a witch herself by all accounts.

Think of this process as being something along the lines of James Joyce creating the fictional character of Leopold Bloom. Who in turn—within the novel—creates Stephen as a *Daemon* of himself. A kind of magical Russian doll created by Joyce. Expressed, and brought into manifestation, within the pages of the novel. Joyce then performs something of a literary version of the *Alchemical Wedding* within the final chapter by transporting his own consciousness into that of Molly, by assuming something of a sacred hermaphrodite in order to understand the effects of her losing a child has upon her sexuality.

This act of Joyce—and the reader—entering the psycho-sexual mind of Molly is later expressed in Joyce's follow-up novel, *Finnegan's Wake.* That being, generating the unbounded space-time and linguistic enchantments of her dreams as the result of her issuing forth the incantation, 'yes I said yes I Will Yes.' during her final orgasm at the end of *Ulysses.* It is no coincidence that Joyce deliberately capitalized the term 'Will' in her final statement within the novel. The pain and suffering of life and love is thus exploded into the cosmos in an act of what can be considered literary *Sex Magic.* By writing the novel *Ulysses*, James Joyce not only resolved his own sexual and psychologically intense relationship with his real-life wife Nora—through the characters and situations contained within the novel—but also created a whole new cultural and even social dynamic for the city he was born in.

The novel's hero, Bloom—as the outsider—represented all the things about Dublin which James Joyce both loved and hated about his native city and homeland. From this paradox, Bloom—along with his fictional protégé Stephen—became a kind of *Daemon* of the *Will* of James Joyce. Both as a real-life husband, and as an Irishman. *Ulysses* has come to be seen as the greatest novel in English literature. Is it any wonder that upon reading *Ulysses*, none other than Aleister Crowley himself proclaimed, "I am convinced personally that Mr. Joyce is a genius all the world will have to recognize." One great magician always recognizes the craft of another. The same process also takes place within the conjuration of sorcery, in that a conscious—self-aware entity or aspect—generates itself alongside the *Will* of the magician. This background entity or process is directly related to the emotional and psychological state of the magician or artist. **The muse you get is not the muse you want. It will be the muse you need.** This is also why sorcery can backfire spectacularly if a curse is placed upon an undeserving individual. The muse of conjuration throws it right back into your face almost like a sports umpire or referee. You are forced into dealing with yourself before you pass the buck on to some other person undeserving of your sorcery. This concept of the shadow being cast by our sorcery was demonstrated in this famous illustration by French ceremonial magician Éliphas Lévi (1810-1875). The graphic also returns us to the concept of honoring our own shadow, so as to understand ourselves as individuals, before we attempt to impose our own *Will* upon the rest of the world. For every benediction, there is a malediction, and *vice versa*.

THE FETCH AND THE DOPPELGANGER

A few years ago, I was walking down a street in Dublin minding my own business. At the time, a certain individual living in New York was constantly on my mind due to some unresolved issue I had with him. The situation affected me greatly. I could not get this person off my mind. I was unable to 'reach out' so as to contact this person. As a result, he was living rent-free inside my thoughts. The rumination was non-stop.

Suddenly, out of the corner of my eye, there comes walking towards me the very person whom I was so psychologically and emotionally preoccupied with. The experience was incredibly startling. My only response was to keep on walking as if I had not noticed him. I am not sure why I did this. It was as much instinct as shock. Yet, at the same time, there was an incredible sensation (within my psyche) that this other person was also aware of my presence. This was made known to me without words or eye contact. It was that person, but not the *same* person. After several months, I received a call from this person telling me he had a very vivid dream in which he saw me walking down a street in Dublin. He correctly named the street and also, and that the dream took place on the same day that I had witnessed his apparent double. I did not tell this person about my own experiences at beholding his double.

In Irish folklore, the magical *Daemon* is referred to as The *Fetch,* and is often a *Doppelganger,* or an apparition of a living individual. The *Fetch* is not a ghost, and this is an important distinction. Within the Irish tradition, a person beholding a *Fetch* is considered cursed or hated by the individual who is the one generating the double. For example, seeing one's mother-in-law when you know she is not in town. Something akin to a full-spectrum psychic attack, in that the person on the end of the psychic attack beholds the physical appearance of the person who has malicious thoughts and intent towards them.

However, I believe this is a simplistic, post-Christian interpretation of the phenomenon designed to stigmatize all witches, druids, as well as all mystically-inclined folk, not to mention the experience itself. In Christianity, there is no room for another wizard on this planet apart from the one who ended up being nailed to a plank in the Middle East during the Roman occupation of Judea. The *Fetch* can also be a sign of the magician having such powerful concentration that they can literally send this background consciousness process of their *Will* beyond them as a *Doppelganger.* Conversely, the same intense *Will* (actively or passively induced) can transport The *Fetch* of another person into one's own space-time environment. The latter is what I believe happened to me on that street in Dublin that afternoon. I was being made aware of just how much background development of my own psychic potential had been occurring during my own interest into magical ritual. It had also taught me a very valuable lesson about controlling my emotions: the dangers of rumination. My psychic footprint was far larger than I had previously realized

IN DREAMS

This is also why—as our psychic footprint, or *charisma* develops—we can also appear in other people's dreams to a very vivid degree. In fact, one of the primary indicators of your growing proficiency as a magician is that more and more people will inform you that you have come to them in their dreams. This nocturnal bi-locational ability is not your internal consciousness leaving your body as such. but rather, the *Fetch* or *Daemon* of yourself is moving through, beyond, and in between space-time. When this occurs, you are becoming closer to a god than the basic mortal you once were. Your literal *charisma*—having the grace of the gods—is developing. Along with this, it will continue after you die.

I discovered this in the early 1990s, while I was subject to an incredible dream, in which I conversed (on numerous subjects) with the poet and magician William Butler Yeats, who had died in 1939. At the time, I had no idea what the voice of Yeats actually sounded like. It was not until I found a cassette recording of him reciting his poem *Under Ben Bulben* that I recognized it as the same accent and tonality of voice he had used in the dream. For some inexplicable reason, this phenomenon is one of the least studied areas of sorcery and witchcraft. This is probably a result of most magicians tending to just accept this background fail-safe and independent muse of the magical operation for what it is, and any examination of the experience being more suited to the worlds of parapsychology and metaphysics. Magicians tend not to interfere with this particular dynamic, background intelligence of their craft. Knowing it exists is good enough for most of them. Even so, we should keep these kinds of 'spin-off' effects (of our magical practice) in mind. Every Thor needs a Loki, as much as every Loki needs a Thor. Every echo began with an initial shout.

"Magick is not created by man, it is a part of man, having its basis in the structure of his brain, his body and his nervous system in their relations to his conceptual universe, the matrix of thought, and of speech, the mother of thought." - Jack Parsons

THE FIVE STAGES OF RITUAL AND FOLK MAGIC

All magical practices, from placing a curse upon an individual to creating a great artwork that will change people's perceptions of themselves and their worldview, adhere to the same basic magical principles. Generally, there are five aspects of sorcery which must be followed in order to bring about the intended specific change within the material universe. These five steps also adhere to the five points of the *Pentagram*, which also represents the five basic elements: air, fire, water and earth, as well *aether.*

All five steps must be followed through. Otherwise, the ritual is left open and its decay will be energetically entangled with that of the magician. Banishment of summoned entities is especially vital. Do not start what you cannot, or will not bring to completion. Accept the outcome of the spell or ritual. Learn from the outcome upon completion. To abandon the ritual before the five stages is well illustrated in the *Thoth Tarot* card, the *Five of Swords,* in which *Gevurah* repels those deemed undeserving. Integration, structure and stabilization has broken down. Like the five fingers on your hands, only five will, and can, suffice. This is not to imply that the process is inherently dangerous. Even if the process fails— once you adhered to the five principles—you have not left the tap running, so to speak. Turn off the energetic flow. This includes self-reflection and honest critique if the ritual has failed. In Éliphas Lévi's *Tetragrammaton Pentagram,* he recreated the design as a symbol of the microcosm. The magician as an expression of the totality of the cosmos.

CHANGE: THE ULTIMATE OBJECTIVE OF THE MAGICIAN

The *Five Principles of Ritual Magic* commonly used are:

(1) *Motivation*

This is the objective itself. The essential and vital expedient which is intended to cause the change required within the material world.

(2) *Ritual*

The action or process implemented in order to bring the outcome into manifestation. Something of a combination of a battle plan and performance.

(3) *Invocation*

This will be the source of a 'higher power' or 'agent' called upon by the magician in order to bring about the desired result. It can be a god, angel or some other higher spiritual power. However, these are ultimately archetypes or names for powerful—yet often little used—aspects of the psyche. This is a highly respectful process. We are not summoning the higher power as our servant. We are invoking this power with humility and great reverence.

In my own case, I often invoke the Macha, also known as *The Sun of Womanfolk*, who, along with her sisters, Badb and Morrigu (Morrigan) comprise the triple battle goddess of the northern half of Ireland. All three are collectively known as the "Morrígna". The reason I call upon the Macha is primarily due to the psychic power force which her archetype still holds—as a colossal charge—within the Irish landscape. Particularly among the megalith-covered landscapes of both County Sligo, where I reside, and especially among the hills and highlands of Ulster to the north.

However, you can use any power force you wish. Some magicians even invoke fictional entities such as Batman. It's your call. Find an archetype, and then bring its psychic power potential into manifestation. However, always make sure to understand the full complexities of the archetype you are working with. This invocation is the compression of the *Will* into something of a projectile that is unleashed as a pure stream of energy towards the intended target.

(4) *Medium*

This is the object or device used to move the *Will* away from the magician, and towards the target or intended outcome. Again, it is both symbolic and/or literal. For example, an intensely passionate oration proclaimed while pointing a wand towards the intended target. The issuing of a curse. The creation of a piece of artwork. A *Sigil*. Propaganda, and so on. It can be anything from a satire—making fun of a famous person—by turning their friends and supporters against them, to a love letter sent to win the heart of a beloved, whom one eventually marries and has children with. When witches of the past boiled various items into the *Medium* of a cauldron, the objects placed into it were totems—or symbolic representations—of certain natural/cosmic powers and forces.

The boiling cauldron itself was a ritualistic performance so as to charge these particular energetic forces into the *Will* of the witches who were performing the ceremony. The act of the boiling cauldron should be considered as being something akin to a star-gate, or portal. A portal for the witches' *Will* to pass through the present limitations of current space-time, and on towards the intended target. It may be viewed as something crude and primitive. However, the witches' *Will*, along with their boiling cauldron, is fundamentally a highly scientific process. One using objects and materials available to them at the time, so as to hack the underlying dynamics of the universe. Your great grandmother's own *Hadron Collider*.

(5) *Ensual*, or the outcome of the magical process.
This is the final act of change. The change within the material world can be anything and everything the magician (reasonably) desires. However, it won't happen instantly, and it won't happen without these five stages being carefully planned and implemented.

WIDENING THE ANCIENT PATH

Although I have written this book as something of a stripped down and philosophically-orientated tome with the intention of opening up a new world of sorcery to the reader, I shall not forgo some of the basic tenets and time-proven methods of conveying the dynamics and processes of the magical craft. I am not entirely reinventing the wheel. However, the tools of the past which have been proven to work are staying in the toolkit. Precisely because they do work. They have been successful for many others, and have enjoyed longevity for this very reason. Hence why ideas of metaphor, allegory, symbolism and archetypes are still so central to the practice of sorcery.

The present level of human consciousness is still very reliant upon metaphor and symbolism in order to convey certain ideas that would otherwise be baffling and complicated. The same processes which worked for the proto-shamanic cultures—who oversaw the creation of the megaliths of the Neolithic period—still work in the modern age. This being due to humans remaining—within the overall spectrum of consciousness—the same type of creature they have been for thousands of years.

Our post-*Enlightenment* conscious and logical minds initially have difficulty comprehending the fuel which makes the star inside us all shine brightly. Metaphor and allegory are useful tools towards this end.

UNTAMED LIGHT

In December 2014, an American research department at Northwestern University captured the precise moment when an egg was fertilized by a sperm by means of photographing a flash of light as the event occurred in real time. Although this 'spark' is believed to be the simultaneous ignition of millions of zinc atoms moving through a living cell structure, the process nonetheless demonstrated the precise moment when a soul—or independent conscious identity—enters into this reality via the portal of human biological procreation. The phenomenon demonstrated that life begins with the manifestation of a luminous presence. We are all stars.

In real time, the Northwestern University research team were able to observe this display of microscopic fireworks—which lasted for over two hours—after the fertilization by the sperm had been initiated. Although the scientists captured the event for the first time, they still could not fully explain the trigger mechanism which causes all this to come about.

It is one thing for it to have been simply a chemical reaction inside cells, but it is another, very different thing entirely, that this display of light eventually develops consciousness. A consciousness and psychic self-awareness that—during further cellular growth and expansion—deepens and continually creates throughout the course of the individual's life. The absolute origin and *ground zero* of this process—the one who turned on the light switch—is still a complete mystery.

THE ETERNAL FLAME

In the case of my own cultural background, one of the great mysteries relating to Irish mythology is the lack of a creation myth. The reason for this is apparent once we look at other Pagan, as well as wider Indo-European spiritual traditions around Europe. It is that there is no beginning nor end to the Pagan Indo-European cosmology, as such. Terminal and fated notions of impending annihilation of biological life—without rebirth or reincarnation—are ideas almost unique to the Abrahamic religions; specifically, Islam and Christianity.

Most people understand this idea—of absolute biological commencement and termination—being represented by the transition from *Genesis* to *Armageddon*. As a result, the Abrahamic religions are among the very few which do not have the hard maxim of reincarnation at their spiritual core. This creates a terrible worldview/collective neurosis within human beings, whereby destruction is always just around the corner in one form or another. Unless, of course, they do everything that the god of the *Bible* and the *Koran* tells them to do. Then they will live in paradise after the destruction.

I must also point out that Judaism, on the other hand, presents something of a far more complex and less fatalistic approach, when one begins to look into the *Kabbalah*. This may also explain why Judaism is the only Abrahamic religion which does not evangelize, while the other Abrahamic religions are consumed with *Crusades* and *Jihad*. There is a type of reincarnation within Judaism known as G*ilgul*. A most interesting idea. Essentially, a person works toward pre-planning their reincarnation during his or her own lifetime. Often, this is undertaken to make amends for mistakes or wrong-doings in this life. As a deep exploration of the *Kabbalah* is outside the pale of this book, nonetheless, I would encourage readers interested in studying the *Kabbalah* to do so, as there is much magical wisdom and insight to be gained in doing this.

There is no start to the universe. There is no end to the universe. It has always existed and it will always exist. The material and organic matter which encapsulates our imperishable underlying spiritual state is, itself, also a continuous event. On this planet, it recycles itself—as seasons and biological cycles—around the spiritual light which is central to these states and experiences. Traditionally, we have been in something of an *Archetypal Entanglement* with these natural cycles, which our ancestors culturally expressed as the gods and goddesses that have emanated from within the various Indo-European mythologies. Thor = thunder, Loki = lightning, Ostara = springtime and Lugh = solar forces, and so on.

However, natural forces—throughout all their phases—always represent a constant rebirth. The underlying light is the essence of the consciousness; and, by extension, is likewise also the essence of the cosmos. It is eternal, and transcends the so-called limitation of matter. European Pagan and heathen spiritual imagery has long represented this symbolic rotation of life and regenerative life forces in terms of the sun-wheel S*wastika,* the *'Celtic Cross',* and so on. At the center of most Pagan and polytheistic spiritual traditions is the idea of this eternal and indestructible circle of existence that is perpetual light. That light being the underlying force of anything and everything.

THE LIGHT BODY

Within most spiritual and esoteric traditions, including the Abrahamic religions (it must be said), human beings are believed to be composed of two states. One being the physical body, and the other being known as the light body. Also referred to as the *auric,* or energetic body, upon which the biology of the person wraps around, and hangs off from. There are numerous interpretations of this idea, ranging from the *auric* body being a ball of light, a silvery thread and even, in some cultures, an identical, non-material double of the person's physical body. Moreover, the most common belief attributed to this universally-accepted *auric* body—regardless of any archetypal or anthropomorphic ideas associated with it —is that it is also capable of leaving the physical body. A process known as *Astral Traveling*, or by means of an *Out of Body Experience* (OBE). However, it still retains a direct connection to the person until the moment of death. At that point, the *auric* body moves on permanently in search of a new life.

LIFE ETERNAL

One of the most conclusive arguments for the survival of human—and other forms of consciousness—following biological death, was accidentally discovered during the early days of *Spiritualism*. When cards with letters written on them were spread around the table, where a *seance* was being conducted, the 'spirits' were then asked to move a glass or planchett of some kind—which the attendees were touching collectively —towards the relevant letters that would spell out the name of the deceased. Or else, they were asked to answer some other specific question(s) put to the spirit. What soon became apparent was that certain spirits could not spell out any words. Or else they just produced nonsense. Eventually, it was realized that the spirits—who could effectively communicate—generally belonged to previously middle class and above individuals, who were actually capable of effective communication only because they were formally educated. They could read and write, in other words. The reverse was also true, with the poor and working class spirits being unable to make effective post-mortal communication, because they were often illiterate. The case for life after physical death only became stronger when—as the public education model spread out from the *Prussian Empire* and onto most of the civilized world—the recently departed (who came from the lower classes) were finally able to then communicate during *Spiritualism* sessions. This was possible for no other reason than they had been taught how to read and write during their mortal lifetime.

In all cases, the recently departed explained that they had left their physical bodies, and were still the same person that they had been while they were alive. They were still able to move around within this reality. Just as they were capable of doing so when they were still alive. The recently departed also stated that their time within this 'ghost' state was temporary. They instinctively knew (or were told) that they had some other places to go to.

In the Victorian era, the assumption was that they were heading for either Heaven or Hell. However, as these spirits were questioned further, far more complex experiences were expressed concerning reincarnation—as well as spending a period of time among idyllic afterlife landscapes— where they underwent a process of considering the course and actions of their previous mortal lives. Purgatory—albeit in a more pleasant and interesting format—was apparently more real than either Heaven or Hell.

When these stories began to emerge and became commonly reported, the *Spiritualism* movement became a target of the established religions. Then came professional hoax exposers, who sought to throw the frauds and sincere mediums into the same public court of ridicule. For the majority of people who attended these *Spiritualism* events, however, the experience was reported as being overwhelmingly positive. Without a doubt, the veracity of life—or rather, the conscious mind—continuing to exist after death was ostensibly proven with the discovery that illiterate spirits could not communicate during seances, while educated ones could. This should have been considered one of the greatest discoveries of all time. The absolute proof that we are made up of both matter and soul. That the soul—along with the personality connected to it—survives biological demise. Predictably, the opposite happened, when the people who found themselves healed by communicating with their late loved ones were ridiculed, while the sincere mediums were either thrown in jail or slandered in the media.

HOW SPIRITUALISM REVIVED SORCERY

Along with the ability to communicate with the recently departed, another dynamic was re-emerging within Western society during the late Victorian era: the potential of communication with human spirits—and other entities—so as to procure information that was otherwise very difficult, or impossible to obtain. This is what really concerned the authorities regarding the success of *Spiritualism* during this period.

It gave back to ordinary people their belief in the supernatural. This was seen as terrifying by the power structures of the time. Any man or woman with the ability to communicate with non-material entities also had the ability to gain information about the ruling classes and what they were up to. Hence, why something of a magical class system (once again) soon emerged, whereby the poor were given rosary beads and prayer, while the elite of society set about their sorcery.

The first great occult revival of the late Victorian era was absolutely a result of the success and grassroots popularity of the *Spiritualism* movement when people—mainly educated and well-off bohemian types —set up or joined existing occult organizations such as the *Golden Dawn*. This also included the more esoteric branches of Freemasonry, as well as Druidry revivalist groups which became popular among the gentry within their large country homes. This popularity for magical practice among the artistic types and the intelligentsia of late Victorian society eventually inspired entire movements such as the *Gaelic Revival* in Ireland, along with the resurgence of folk sorcery and occultic traditions in Germany and much of central Europe. In Ann Saddlemyer's book—*Becoming George: The Life of Mrs. WB Yeats*—the wife of the Irish poet and occultist William Butler Yeats is shown as the kind of woman typical of this transition period between the *Spiritualism* movement and the late Victorian occult revival. Her famous husband himself stated in the foreword to his own book, *A Vision,* how his wife

George (Georgina) had astounded the poet with her abilities of *Automatic Writing*, *Trace Speech*, and how she even manifested "spirits". These entities then supplied WB Yeats with the metaphors that became central to his own magical poetry.

The respectable bohemian society of the era would meet in order to discuss the connection between the arts and the occult. Intense debates on the meanings of Egyptian mythology, in particular, seems to have captivated these gatherings. Experiments into psychic abilities, *Table Rapping* and *Automatic Writing* soon led to many joining the existing occult orders, or led to the creation of new magical and esoteric ceremonial groups. The connection between the arts and the occult among the middle and upper classes was the impetus for this fashionable mysticism.

DANGEROUS PARLOR, AND OTHER GAMES?

However, there are—as we shall see later—certain risks associated with entities or 'demons' taking something of an interest in these magical activities. In fact, one of the reasons formal ceremonial sorcery became so complex and ritualistic was due to increasing safeguards needed to ensure that these entities were kept safely at a distance so as not to interfere with the performance of the rites. Or especially, avoiding any unwanted psychic disruptions afterwards. Weak-minded individuals—or people tortured by neurosis and doubts—attending ceremonial sorcery rituals are often seized upon by entities. Entities which had either been deliberately summoned, or had taken an interest in the proceedings.

DEMONIC LURES

Some pathological magicians go even further, in that they delibertely bring along certain types of insecure and damaged individuals so as to act as lures for the invocation of these entities. A demon loves nothing more than a tortured failed poet with a bad opium habit. Naturally, this is extremely unethical, and as late as the 1990s, disturbed teens—in places such as Long Island, New York—became pathologically inclined towards inviting a certain type of vulnerable or insecure peer into the woods for this specific purpose. These gullible lures would be taken to make-shift 'satanic' ceremonies (in woodland locations) for the purpose of terrorizing—and even murdering ('sacrificing')—these unfortunate young people. Drug and alcohol abuse also tended to be central to such tragic and moronic rituals. Although I would be the last person to feel the need for a *Satanic Panic* within society now and again, there is certainly some truth in the notion that suburban teens—as well as drug dealers and other criminal gangs—dabbling in the magical arts very often leads to horrific outcomes. Sorcery—like bad poetry—can be dangerous in the wrong hands.

Aleister Crowley ostensibly used Victor Neuburg for such a purpose in the Sahara Desert in December 1909, when he summoned 'the dweller in the abyss' known as Choronzon. Although Neuburg was never the same person ever again following this ritual, it should be pointed out that Crowley did take suitable precautions to ensure their safety by employing a complex ritual and ceremonial set-up. The risks associated with summoning mighty demons—or performing complex rituals without suitable precaution—can have personal, as well as socially damaging effects. Although Crowley understood precisely what he was doing—as well as the risks involved—far too many are willing to open the gates without knowing how to slam them shut afterwards. It would not be unreasonable, for example, for some to speculate that the pathological ascendancy which took stewardship of the *Häxan* magical revival of Germany—during the *Volkish* movement of the Victoria era—eventually evolved into the Third Reich—and from this, the horrors of *World War Two*.

As with any cultural mass movement, the quality of the craft deteriorates in direct proportion to the ascendancy of the demonic/*daemonic* forces which it can unleash. Some have even speculated that the previous *Great War/World War One* itself may have been a result of using the emerging radio technologies of the period in an attempt to communicate with spirits. Thus leading to the opening up of a demonic floodgate, so to speak, until the technology was put to more prosaic use. Likewise, it would not be outside the bounds of possibility to also suggest that the respectable magical and occult fashionistas of Victorian London deliberately unleashed socially damaging entities—in order to affect society as a whole—during their ritual sorcery performances. Sometimes, the controllers can find themselves being the ones being controlled. Which is also why I would advise people with addictive personalities to refrain from ceremonial magic, and most certainly to not get drunk or stoned during the actual rituals. For all the hype surrounding Aleister Crowley's unbridled enthusiasm for alcohol and drugs, I can assure the reader that the *'Great Beast 666'* would have been very sober when embarking upon complex or risky rituals.

One could even ponder if this highly publicized love of Crowley's for substance abuse was a method—he was clandestinely using—so as to lure in a certain type of 'demonically receptive' human bait into his circle, so to speak. The ambitiously hedonistic 'willing fools', captivated by the graffiti which Crowley had painted upon the wall of his *Abbey of Thelema* in Cefalù, which proclaimed, "Stab your demonic smile to my brain. Soak me in cognac, cunt and cocaine." People forget that Crowley was also a supreme trickster, and there was no shortage of impulsive types allowing themselves to be tricked by the Loki from Lemmington Spa.

All risky magical business aside, the artistic and bohemian set who filled organizations such as the *Golden Dawn*—as well as other magical societies—played an integral role in not only the revival of magical practices (from the Middle Ages and the *Renaissance)*, but also refined and embellished these rites for the post-*Enlightenment* age. The popular stereotype of the eccentric individual—performing extremely complex arcane rituals—while also being the guardians of the craft, very much took root during this period. The complexity of these rituals was also proven to be a valuable tool in scaring off the more pathologically minded and unstable individuals from invoking instant magical and supernatural powers for their own control and manipulation of others. Sadly, they still have organized religions for this. The fictional Mr. Mocata—the sinister *Black Magic* cult leader in Dennis Wheatley's book *The Devil Rides Out*—remains an enduring image within the public consciousness. For all the negative portrayals, as well as cultural ridicule which the magicians and occult organizations of the late Victoria era have leveled towards them, there is no doubt that the popularity of magic and the occult today would not have happened—to the degree that it has— without these Victorian and Edwardian parlor room sorcerers.

THE CUNNING MEN AND WOMEN

Yet, while sorcery circles and occult rituals became a popular novelty—if not a fad—among the upper echelons of society, across the vast Victorian metropolis of London, among the poor and downtrodden of the East End and other poorer parts of the city, an occult revival wasn't necessary, as the *Folk Magic* traditions of these communities never went away to begin with. Away from the *Regency* streets and tree-lined avenues of affluent bohemians discovering that material reality was—to a degree—optional, the dank and red brick-lined streets and alleys of Spitalfields, Limehouse, Kentish Town and Whitechapel were home to a kind of urban shaman known as the *Cunning Folk*.

These sorcery practitioners had evolved out of the social and cultural ruins of the *English Civil War,* as well as the subsequently puritanical Cromwell era. *Cunning Folk* were the fine line between sorcery, medicine and barbers, having all of these pursuits blurred within a field known as *Physick*. These *Cunning Folk* were the sole guardians of magical texts for the creation of *Charms* and conjurations, designed almost exclusively for the purpose of healing. This also extended to healing sick animals, the locating of lost or stolen goods, protection from hexes and the *Evil Eye* (*Apotropaic Magic*), to wooing a lover, and finding the location of some buried treasure. Astrology and divination services were also made available by these metropolitan witches. All this witchcraft and sorcery was thriving among the poor of London in spite of King James I and his oppressive and hysterical *Witchcraft Act 1563*. An *Act* enacted for the primary purpose of keeping sorcery out of the hands of the peasantry. Despite the mundane and sometimes crass objectives of these blasphemous conjurations, the magical texts of the London *Cunning Folk* demonstrated a surprisingly sophisticated level of occult practice. While the wealthy of London looked towards the secrets of the ancient Egyptians, Tibetan and Hindus, right under their very noses—and only a few miles away—was a complex tradition of socially-ingrained sorcery that was deeply entrenched within the daily lives of the urban poor. A part of every day existence as much as *Folk Magic* and witchcraft existed in the rural countryside far beyond the urban smog.

THE CIRCLE FOR RAISING Oberion.

The invocation of the 'fairy king' Oberion—as a multidimensional resource at the disposal of the *Cunning Folk*—was commonly undertaken so as to obtain information from the 'spirit' world. This was achieved by means of creating *Oberion's Seal* upon the occasion of the first moon. This procuring of information—concerning future events and hidden objects—was an essential part of the *Cunning Folk*'s craft. While the magical orders of the upper classes concerned themselves with the magical rituals of Atlantis and Ancient Egypt, the sorcery of the poor and downtrodden was very much rooted in folk and early Pagan traditions of the society in which they were based. Ironically, this made it somewhat more authentic, too.

Sorcery functions best within a very real localized cultural sense. The local environment—as well as the ancestral memory of the particular tribe or culture connected to it—makes their native, magical heritage resonate more deeply within the tribe. Something of a racial-magic familiarity of sorts. This is why I have personally seen so many Irish-Americans (and other members of the Irish diaspora) be literally 'switched on' upon bringing them to an ancient sacred site here in Ireland.

The chattering classes generally had no direct connection to Ancient Egypt. It was very much a case of cultural appropriation within a magical sense. One of the *Golden Dawn*'s most influential members, William Butler Yeats, would eventually turn to the Pagan and folk sorcery traditions of his native Ireland. Yeats achieved spectacular results in doing so with the literal invocation of the *1916 Easter Rebellion* in Dublin as a result of his mystical play *Kathleen Ni Houlihan*. The play's performance at the Abbey became a very real ritual which led to the uprising. Many of the central figures—during the actual military engagement—were involved in the Abbey Theater itself, and numerous insurgents had attended the play before taking up arms against the British Empire. While many of the working class rebels took up arms to free Ireland, little did they know that the final spark which sent them into battle was deeply rooted in the magic of the artists, playwrights and poets of bohemian Dublin. In many ways, this magical class divide perfectly illustrates the conundrum concerning sorcery and occultic acceptance within Western society. The tradition of folk magical rites among the population at large has shown remarkable resilience and tenacity to survive and thrive right up to the present era of the Internet and mass communication, Sorcery just won't go away, regardless of how many times people invoke the Arthur C. Clarke popular quote about advance technologies being indistinguishable from magic. Even if Clarke's quote was correct, it only solidifies the overall legitimacy of the magical process as outlined within the theme of this book.

THE OCCULT AND ESPIONAGE

The official bodies, institutions and bureaucracies which mandate our lives also have other reasons for constantly encouraging the general public to ridicule ideas of magic and sorcery. Occult organizations—as well as individuals involved in the magical arts—have long been prime recruits for the intelligence services. From the time of John Dee, this association has been self-evident to the point whereby it is hardly concealed. The main tool in 'hiding' these high-flying occultists is official ridicule of any ideas surrounding the plausibility of magic and the affairs of state. For example, all the scholarly biographies of John Dee treat his deep involvement with magic and sorcery as something of a minor aspect of his life. The same situation can also be found in academic biographies of both William Butler Yeats and Sir Issac Newton.

The literature of Dennis Wheatley was essentially a body of work surrounding fictionalized 'whistle-blowing' concerning the mystique of both espionage and the occult. Wheatley was more than aware of the symbiotic nature of both within military and government. He was an establishment insider with a knowledge of the British 'deep state' workings and machinations during the *Second World War*. Wheatley's knowledge of the occult was hardly fleeting or superficial, and this includes his profound understanding of *Oriental Mysticism,* outlined in the pages of his novels, such as *Strange Conflict*.

MAGI SPY VERSUS MAGI SPY

A magician makes an ideal spy. Their knowledge of ciphers, secret codes, mind tricks, deception, 'invisibility', human psychology—as well as the usefulness of not being taken seriously by the general public—are precisely the reasons why the intelligence agencies recruit occultists. Aleister Crowley himself was almost certainly a British spy. Frankly speaking, it would be incredible if he was never approached for recruitment. This is what most certainly saved him from a *high treason* charge upon his returning to Great Britain (from New York) following the end of the hostilities of the *Great War*. Crowley's—at times comical—pro-German and Irish Republican sympathies were almost certainly a cover story for his spying activities while he was working for a pro-German newspaper.

University of Idaho Professor of History, Richard B. Spence, in his paper, *Secret Agent 666: Aleister Crowley and British Intelligence in America, 1914-1918*, proves—almost conclusively—that the 'Great Beast' was a deeply embedded British spy. His activities extended to joining Irish freedom groups in the USA, and even went as far as declaring an '*Irish Republic and War Against England*' on July 3, 1915, during an almost surrealist fiasco which took place at the base of the *Statue of Liberty* on Ellis Island in New York Harbor. This alone should have been enough to land him in prison upon his return home, considering that war broke out in Ireland almost a year later.

During this period, Crowley was more of a jester than a spy, and this is what almost certainly saved him from detection by the groups he had infiltrated. Was Crowley a hypocrite for doing this? Not at all. Magicians have no 'patriotism', as such. They understand that existence transcends any notions of loyalty towards any government or political cause. Magicians operate within a world of their own making, and, in many ways, this is what also makes them the ultimate anarchists.

To magicians such as Crowley, being a spy would have also been exciting. As well as an opportunity to refine the magical craft into new directions, there would also be financial and other incentives to add to the appeal. Crowley was not the first British occultist to have infiltrated the Irish freedom struggle during the late Victorian and early 20th century. Irish freedom groups in the USA were well aware of this 'invisibility', mainly due to the number of occultists on the side of Irish freedom working on behalf of that objective. *The Golden Dawn,* for example, played a central role in the restoration of the Irish national and cultural revival. So the totality of occultism was well known on all sides. Creating this level of paranoia among such groups is a magical spell in and of itself. Disrupting agendas and operations. Causing fractures among members to the point whereby this fear of 'occult' individuals functioning within the group takes primary focus away from the main cause of the group itself. Not much had changed since Saint Patrick and 'invisible' druids.

MAGICAL HIGH SOCIETY

Naturally, any knowledge of links between espionage and the occult would have only been privy to the upper echelons of society, while the majority of the population remained woefully ignorant of what really went on within the deep state. This esoteric and spiritual class system also serves as a suitable metaphor to illustrate the concept of the two states of every person: the official physical body, and the unofficial *auric* body.

This is precisely what the affluent Victorian occultists such as George Yeats and her esteemed husband were searching for: a mystical authenticity, and it was no surprise that such ideas took root among the artistic communities of the era. As they would once again—later on in history—as the *Beat Generation* and *Post-Modernist* poets and writers of the 1950s such as William S. Burroughs embarked upon their own exploration into ritual sorcery and the occult. In every case, the search is to establish the existence of the non-material aspect of the human experience, and then, upon verifying this, to find something useful to do with it.

THE LIGHT FROM WITHIN

One magical maxim which has always been present within all cultures and spiritual traditions is that of a supernatural light—and later, magnetism and electricity—being universally central to this personal magical, or mystical potential. This light was also seen as a representation of the soul or *auric* body. The magical and spiritual dimension within us, being symbolical, and literally represented by light. The religious paintings of the halo of Jesus Christ, for example, or the glow surrounding depictions of the Virgin Mary, and so on. We see this effect portrayed in both Christian and Hindu art.

These are essentially accurate artistic representations of the *auric* body if we could all see it with our own eyes. Unfortunately, the Abrahamic religions have conditioned people into believing that this 'inner light' is something that comes with a dogmatic admission price, based almost exclusively upon self-denial and self-loathing. When in fact, we are all born with this *auric* state within us. This is a powerful spiritual idea. Not only in Western Pagan and heathen spiritual traditions, but also in the ancient Egyptian, Hindu and seemingly numerous other spiritual and mystical traditions who all share the same basic underlying mystical ideas relating to the inner magical light as being the 'authentic' state of the individual. It was also during the late Victorian occult revival that scientists began to seriously study the idea of an energetic or luminous field surrounding the human body which existed outside of the limitations of normal sensory perception. It had been accepted that objects such as certain stones, crystals, as well as some types of bio-luminescent animals, fungi and insects contained what was referred to as an 'odic' force. An idea, which, in time, became central to the popular revival of Germanic Häxan sorcery as the early 20th century began.

CAPTURING THE INSIDE STAR

Following on from the work and experiments into the field of "electrography" developed in 1889 by Czech B. Navratil, and later, in 1896, when H. Baraduc successfully produced electrographs of hands and leaves, a growing interest in the phenomenon of living objects emitting a field of light around them captured the imagination of both scientists and the general public. This interest only deepened when, in 1898, a Russian engineer named Yakov Narkevich-Iodko presented a spectacular display of electrography to the *Russian Technical Society*. Eventually, the scientific study into this unknown force contained within living things—

and even rocks with quartz or other crystal seams—developed in tandem with the popularity of both *Spiritualism* and the occult revival of the period. In 1911, the first images of this energy field were captured on a device known as a *Kilner Screen,* named after the scientist who invented it.

The most profound observation made with the *Kilner Screen* was that this energy field—which surrounded people—varied from person to person. More interestingly, these variations and fluctuations were observed as part of a range—expressed as different levels of luminescence— irrespective of the age and physical health of the individuals tested. A subject who was an elderly female near the end of her life could be capable of producing a stronger energetic field than a healthy and fit young male in the prime of his life. The underlying generation of the field—along with what made it weaker or stronger—was a contentious topic of debate among scientists and physicians of the era. However, not among occultic and more esoterically-inclined groups such as Theosophists. The power of the generated field was seen as being directly connected to the spiritual or magical power of the individual.

Eventually, by means of a series of sensational discoveries happening simultaneously in both Czechoslovakia and Russia, this led to the development of what became known as *Kirlian Photography,* after an electrical engineer named Semyon Kirlian, who in 1938—while observing the use of electric current on patients at a hospital while they were undergoing treatment—noticed, along with his wife, that a neon-like glow emanated from the skin of the people being treated.

After twenty years of intense and meticulous research—endorsed and funded by the Soviet government—the Kirlians reported the findings of their research. By the late 1960s, their work also became something of a minor sensation in the West when the "Kirlian Aura" became widely known beyond the *Iron Curtain*. Eventually, a research program was set up at UCLA in the United States to evaluate and replicate Kirlian's research. Predictably, this was abruptly shut down in 1979. However, the cat was out of the bag—in that the *auric* body of all living things had been scientifically verified—and this cat was never going to go back in. No matter how much, or how frequently, the research was ignored or dismissed as 'pseudo-scientific'.

PROJECTING OF FORCES DURING MAGICAL STATES

This *auric* light also allows the non-material attributes—contained within a living organism—the means to move beyond the physical mass which surrounds it. This is then connected to experiences outside the space-time dimension of the bodily shell (so to speak), and is also in direct contact with the mysterious and unknown forces of the universe, acting as something of an interface, which then impacts upon material matter. This is why strong Kirlian fields of energy can also be detected around 'sacred' objects—such as holy relics—which people have venerated and placed their psychic energy into. Such sacred objects and locations then become something akin to a psychic battery.

Some carrier or conduit is responsible for these transmissions of psychic energy, and this, I believe, is the so-called *Dark Matter/Energy* which makes up most of the universe. Our consciousness and psychic states press upon this force, and then this moves or alters matter—and even perceptions of reality—on the other end of the process, where the *Will* is being projected. An abyss of unseen gods and forces performing the task of middle men, between that of the *Will* and the intended outcome. The author Karl W. Luckert termed this the *'Turnaround Realms'*, and used the analogy of the ancient Egyptian gods of Horus, Thoth and Anubis being the 'accessible' entities which can act as something of a go-between, connecting humans to the ultimate forces of creation. The enablers of human magical workings.

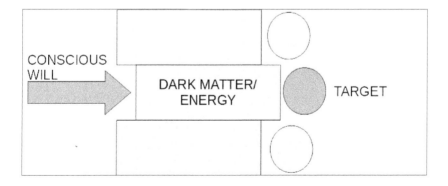

CULTIVATING YOUR MAGICAL INNER STAR

We can all perform exercises and rituals which can help restore and regenerate these magical abilities within us as individuals. Artists use this ability all the time. The intensity placed within the act of creating a poem, painting, novel or screenplay can result in enormous changes within culture and society as a whole, not just the creation of new artistic and cultural movements derived from any stylistic or aesthetic gravitas contained and projected from the artistic work. Vincent van Gogh's use of brushstrokes eventually inspired exploration into new scientific fields. In the case of his painting *Starry Night*, this included discoveries within particle physics, along with inspiring new theories concerning the science of turbulence and flow research. This 'insight' is ultimately derived— and manifested—from the process of practice and refinement. What works for the painter continually painting, or the actor rehearsing their lines over and over again, works for the magician developing their craft. Tragically for Vincent van Gogh, he was a Western shaman who found himself born at the wrong time. Or maybe it was, in fact, the correct time...

PERSONAL SACRED MAGICAL JOURNAL

Powering one's *Will* into a pure stream of energy can be cultivated and refined by keeping a secret journal of your dreams, inclinations, desires and intentions, writing them down as candidly and honestly as you can. Doing so will act as something of an amplifier of your own magical charge. A sacred logbook of your own psyche, so to speak. Include images and simple drawings—to symbolize your thoughts—so as to transfer complex personal sensations and desires into these symbols. If some unusual design or shape appears in a dream, or just arrives in your *mind's eye* out of the blue, then make note of it. Meditate upon this symbol. Especially before you go to sleep at night. These books will eventually become a kind of portal into higher states of consciousness and sensory awareness. The *Dark Matter/Energy* of the universe unfolds its potential into your life (via the symbols transmitted from your subconscious) and you'll soon discover that reality becomes far more optional than you were led to believe. Monitor the themes and contents of your dreams. Do not attempt to over-analyze the dreams each morning. Allow them to create a two-way conversation with your subconscious, and pay attention to them. Write them down, even if they do not make sense or they disturb you. In time, you will begin to have prophetic dreams, and that which you desired—with great passion—begins to manifest into your life. **Most importantly of all is to keep this personal book private and treat it with great reverence.** It is, after all, your passport to godhood.

RITUALISTIC SELF-SACRIFICE

Returning once again to the concept of the sun's fire being present within trees, I would like to illustrate how an entire landscape became something of a personal mega-ritual for me at a point in my life (2008) when I felt had no other option left for personal self-development. A 'guided' ritual which successfully allowed a psychic block to be freed up within me. There was a large forested area near where I live—made up of tightly-packed *Leylandii Cypress* trees—in which I spent many hours wandering and thinking. The *Leylandii Cypress* is not native to Ireland, and so the woodlands created from them can be something of a desert. Even so, within the silence of the forested area, I found it useful for my own contemplation and solitude. Planted in the 1960s, the trees had reached maturity, and were being felled for pulpwood. These fast-growing hybrids had been originally planted as an experiment to drain vast quantities of groundwater from the surrounding boglands, making them accessible for grazing livestock. Having visited the interior of this forest many times and observed what a sterile, barren wasteland lay within its shade, I was pleased to see the hundreds of giant trees being cut down. Many were falling of their own accord and were becoming increasingly dangerous, not to mention increasingly depressing to behold.

A few days later—after the forestry machines had done their work—I returned to see the devastated wasteland where the forest of highly-acidic trees had been. To my great surprise, I was overcome by what I can only describe as a profoundly spiritual experience. For the landscape I beheld before me was—symbolically—myself looking back at me. At that time, I had reached a dead-end in my own creative life, and I felt deeply uninspired and lost. My previous art business had fallen apart due to the recession caused by the international banking crisis of the period, and the future—while not looking hopeless—was not providing me with any foreseeable positive outcome ahead. I was looking at an allegory of myself. A former landscape of utilitarian means, now obsolete and unappealing.

As I wandered around the hundreds of tree stumps, amid the vast carpet of stripped branches that had been violently ripped off—during the heavy machinery tree-felling methods—I could sense the shock within the landscape itself. It was a mirror of how I was feeling myself at the time within my own consciousness. For some inexplicable reason—which I now understand the powerful significance of—I began to pick up certain branches and started to create sculptures of Pagan gods and supernatural animals. Twisting branches here and there, and interlacing them around one another in an attempt to bring something interesting to the bleak landscape. Some of these sculptures were as large as three meters high. With each one I created, I felt my internal psychic forces—which had been stagnant up until that point—begin to move very slowly within me once again.

I was generating gods; or rather, I was calling upon (invoking) the higher forces of my own ancestral archetypal forces present within me, and within the environment. Both the landscape and I became involved in something of a symbiotic dance of emerging co-dependency and creative regeneration. Sorcery was unfolding...

It was also around this time I was taking an interest in Nordic mythology and comparing it with deities and archetypes within Irish mythology. Casting the deeply Christianized editorialized versions of these stories to one side, it soon became apparent to me that the Irish god Lugh and the Nordic god Loki were probably rooted in the same primal entity. Or, at the very least, derived from a much more ancient proto-shamanic tradition representing similar archetypal forces. Our ancient ancestors considered the fire from the sun—as well as lightning—to be of the same cosmic origin. We know that in the Norse *Eddas*, Thor (the thunder god) chases Loki and, as thunder follows lightning, Loki therefore is absolutely representative of lightning. Lightning itself is unpredictable and can strike anywhere and unexpectedly. Just like Loki. While within the Irish mythology, Lugh is often compared to being a solar deity within ancient Ireland. Lugh is also known as *Lugh Lámfada*—which translates as 'his long arm'—and may well have been the fork of lightning reaching down from the sun (from behind the clouds) and striking upon trees. Both Lugh and Loki are likely to be derived from the Indo-European root 'leuk-' which describes the 'flash of light'. As I set about building my tree sculptures, these were the kinds of thoughts and ideas which were filling my mind at the time.

THE INVOCATION OF THE FIRE GODS

As the first summer passed, I noted with disappointment how, apart from my animal and humanoid branch sculptures, the landscape had been as dead as ever. No bio-diversity of any manner, and this was coupled with a strange, and somewhat sinister 'otherworldly' sense of location, like *The Dead Marshes* of J. R. R. Tolkien's *Middle Earth* sagas. There had been almost no wildlife which had settled upon the highly-acidic landscape where the felled trees had been. Nothing. Even a few blades of grass were finding it near impossible to survive. The effect upon the landscape could be comparable to that of an industrial accident.

In October 2008, an exceptionally dry period of warm weather had turned the brittle carpet of fallen *Leylandii Cypress* branches and numerous stumps into a landscape of kindling. It wanted to be engulfed in fire. In the absence of Loki, it wanted me to unleash it. So I took it upon myself to burn the entire landscape—wood sculptures and all—into soot and ash. This would address the *pH* imbalance in the soil, and create a living landscape once more. Making sure there would be no damage to either private property, livestock or wildlife (there was neither around), I set an enormous fire at the location on *Samhain* eve as the sun was setting. The all-engulfing flames shot high into the air and filled the entire region of south Sligo with black smoke. Creating a spectacular, ritualized blood red sunset—filled with a myriad of simulacra-generated faces and supernatural forms—within the moving, swirling plumes of smoke and dancing flames. These simulacra all meandered up into the evening sky as if they were being released from their bondage. It was a thrilling and terrifying experience all at once. At one point, it seemed as if the whole world was about to go up in flames. Then it dawned on me that this was, in fact, what I was doing: burning my own inner world up within these flames. Sacrificing the old me, and all the dead wood—within my psyche —so that new energies and creativity could flow into and from me. My emotional state had reached such levels during this ritualized inferno that are nearly impossible to express, and it created a profoundly emotional charge within me. By the following morning, the entire landscape had become a vista of undulating gray and black ash. The fallen branches were no more, and the stumps of the old trees were smoldering amid the damp morning fog into non-existence. Then, as the rain began to fall, I walked away and allowed Winter to do the rest.

The following Spring, the landscape literally exploded into life with every species of native wild flora and fauna of the region, painting the environment as if it were a freshly primed canvas. Ponds filled with frogs, and all manner of birds to prey upon them. On a landscape where previously not even flies would trespass, now deer were present. The stags' mighty antlers signaling the return of Cernunnos. The ultimate validation of my setting fire to the barren landscape. The ancient archetypes and totems of the landscape had returned. The transformation was thrilling to behold and all this, that I had conjured into manifestation.

At the same time the native landscape was restored, my creativity—in the form of my own *inner fire*—came back with a vengeance. I began painting constantly. I wrote a best-selling book. New doors of opportunity opened and amazing people came into my life. All of which was taking place—in tandem—with the once dead landscape returning to all its glory by means of me having literally invoked Loki and Lugh by 'releasing the lightning' within the remains of the trees.

I had also magically released the lightning inside myself. This was by means of throwing myself (symbolically) into the sacrificial fires in order to burn a new version of myself into existence. It worked. Within a few years, a forestry company had purchased the former government-owned woodland, and began planting new trees made up exclusively of native Irish species such as Oak, Hazel and Ash. The trees of our ancient European ancestors that formed the groves in which the druids worked their own craft. It had been the sterile landscape, representing my creative needs: by invocation of Loki and Lugh, I had conjured a new living landscape—along with a new creative me—into existence. I also learned a valuable lesson about the practice of magic. You can create your own bespoke rituals using what the cosmos provides you with when you need it. This is why it exists. The magical circle which I had created was designed to restore the cycles of the natural world as they were meant to be. In the process, the same cycle had been restored within my own psyche.

REINCARNATION

This is also why Pagan traditions subscribe to the notion of reincarnation. One is more inclined to take care of a world that one will eventually return to. If one believes that they are destined to the idiotic eternal Christian afterlife of a white gown and a pair of wings, then what happens down here on this planet is irrelevant. The same is true for atheists who see nothing beyond themselves. Hence, why Transhumanism has become their own brand of de-facto *Black Magic*. Magic is always a sympathetic reflection of the cyclical nature of the cosmos. This is the circle from which creative forces regenerate and restore themselves.

Another manner of making Characters, delivered by Cabalists.

Amongst the Hebrews I finde more fashions of Characters, whereof one is moſt ancient, *viz.* an Ancient writing which *Moſes*, and the Prophets uſed, the form of which is not raſhly to be diſcovered to any ; for thoſe letters which they uſe at this day, were inſtituted by *Eſdras*. There is alſo a-mongſt them a writing which they call Celeſtiall, becauſe they ſhew it placed and figured amongſt the Stars, no otherwiſe then th...

MAGICK

The spelling of 'magick' with a 'k' dates back to the 16th century and can be found in the works of Heinrich Cornelius Agrippa within his hugely influential *Three Books on Occult Philosophy*.

Magick with the 'k' spelling was reintroduced by Aleister Crowley in his book *Magick In Theory and Practice* in which he stated that the 'k' spelling was to distinguish ritual and ceremonial magick from the magic within folklore and that of stage magicians. However, how one decides to spell the term is a personal preference.

| *Tau* | *Shin* | *Res* | *Kuff* | *Zade* | *Pe* | *Ain* | *Samech* |

Aleph

Cheth

ICONS AND EFFIGIES

The role which quartz plays within the great ancient megalithic sites of the world has always greatly interested me. The numerous and seemingly "impossible" giant stones and monoliths which baffles present-day science and engineering. They simply cannot adequately explain how these immense stones were quarried—let alone transported—into specific locations. Often across long distances of less than ideal terrain. Stones so huge that most modern construction machinery cannot move or position them into the arrangements and locations our Neolithic ancestors could apparently manage with such ease. Something else beyond vast human resources—being whipped into obedience—was behind the construction of these sacred sites.

What if the light bodies, or energetic unseen forces of consciousness of our ancient ancestors during orchestrated rituals—as has been suggested by Colin Wilson—were able to interface with the quartz (or other forces) contained within these giant stones, to simply move them at will? Herding the giant quartz-laden megaliths as would a farmer herd cattle. If this is the case, then could we assume that the consciousness of ancient peoples was very different than our own?

They were people just like us, of course. However, the parts of their psyches not obsessed with sports, celebrity scandals, bank loans and social status, were instead primed towards a more magical sense of self-identity. Perhaps, infused with this sense of personal magical potential, could they move matter and forces beyond themselves—by means of their personal and collective *Will*—simply by assuming this magical state and acting upon it?

If so, then this next question must also be asked: how did we, as modern humans, lose this magical ability? How come our ancient ancestors had such a relationship with the properties contained within stone so as to seemingly perform very real miracles? This is why I, myself, have had a personal obsession with these 'sacred sites' for as long as I can remember. Our ancient ancestors would appear to have had easier access to magic. Why don't we have this today? And where has this magical self-identity gone?

There are numerous theories which have been proposed to suggest a reason for our modern consciousness losing these abilities. From exterior damage caused by everything from a great global catastrophe, to humans being deceived or damaged by non-human entities such as demons, djinn or other ultra-terrestrials—as John Keel, author of *The Mothman Prophecies* termed them—which moved the human mind away from a state of magical free association, and on to the creation of the individual and the highly-personalized ego as a necessary survival mechanism. A view held among some Neo-Pagan groups is the notion of this magic power having been taken over and corrupted by a pathological priest class who intended to use it to enslave humanity, only for their dark sorcery to damage the very fabric of this reality and leading us all to where we are now as a species. At the very least—considering the relationship the elites of today have with ritual and ceremony—perhaps this theory is not so far off the mark.

THE SORCERY OF STONES

Stones are regarded as dead objects by mainstream science. Petrified repositories of ancient life forms and environments. About as far from the requirements needed for developing and holding consciousness as one could possibly imagine. Yet many minerals do contain complex forms of energy. Coal, for example, holds the energy of the ancient past in the form of combustible chemicals. What other forces—not merely geothermal—could be contained within rocks and minerals? From the dawn of history, sorcery, religion and supernatural forces have been intrinsically linked to stones and stone structures. It could be argued that the first and most enduring symbol of humanity's connection with the divine is stone objects. Long before we venerated iconic and zoomorphic representations of deities and supernatural beings, we communicated with the simulacra-laden gods of certain stones. It is hardly surprising, either. Consider the naturally occurring stones which possess unusual qualities, such as the remarkable boulders of the Odenwald forest region of southern Germany, with their unusual magnetic and other properties. Strange effects which I have witnessed (and felt) firsthand and up close. Anomalies which can send compasses into a spin, and complex electronic devices and GPS technologies into chaos. These stones of the Odenwald are still used by witches and other ceremonial magical groups during *Walpurgis* and *Samhain* for this very reason. The forests and mountains of the Odenwald are alive with a magical and folkloric archetypal richness and tradition, and all of this is derived from the very real magical rock formation of the region.

One of the strangest phenomenon recorded is that of rocks moving under their own power. From Death Valley in California, to the *Trovants*—or the 'living stones'—of central and southern Romania. These *Trovants* grow like plants, can move from location to location, and even appear to also procreate and multiply. Like plants, the *Trovants* stones will begin to grow when heavy spring rains arrive, and they can develop from small rocks into huge boulders. They are basically just sandstone in nature. However, they contain growth rings inside them that are very similar to tree rings. Not only are these *Trovants* very literally 'alive'; many have been observed and recorded while moving across the countryside by their own freewill.

We are talking about living, sandstone boulders. The complete inability for modern science to understand how these stones are actually 'alive' is one of the primary reasons they are so little known or discussed outside of Romania. Scientists simply cannot and will not try to explain how they live, grow and move, while the professional debunkers would probably have nervous breakdowns even knowing that they exist. The implication of their existence impacts greatly upon just about every facet of science. Even without the remarkable 'living' or self-propelling moving stones of California and Romania, many cultures even go further, and have a belief that humans are spiritually connected to stones, and that they can also communicate with them. Long before humans domesticated animals, we appear to have had a very close and magical relationship with stones. Why is this? Is this due to unique properties within stone which the humans of the past could access and even communicate with?

THE LITERAL FREEMASONRY

John Foster Forbes, the legendary Scottish archaeological maverick, believed—and in the years since his heyday has been proven correct—that the people of pre–history were far more sophisticated, cultured and technologically adept than have been portrayed by academia. That something of an injustice—which results from this narrow and simplistic, if not bigoted view—robs the people of the ancient past of their own dignity. Added to this injustice, we of the present, likewise, have no pride in the achievements of our ancestors.

Central to the lives of these ancient cultures was a universally-accepted, deeply spiritual and symbolic connection to stones. Stones were vital to their magical and cultural existence, and not just exclusively connected to astronomical observations and seasonal cycles. Although this was a major factor, too. What made Forbes truly visionary in his work was that he implemented a holistic methodology of incorporating—along with archaeology and anthropology—data collected from folklore, superstition, customs and mythology, in order to decode and reveal the evolution and eventual dispersion of aboriginal Europeans of the Atlantic regions during pre–history. Even today, this is considered a radical approach by the mainstream historians. Yet it has been shown time and time again to be a valuable source of information gathering, best suited towards uncovering new revelations concerning the ancient past. Something of a magical archaeology.

OUR ANCESTORS' SORCERY STILL SPELLBIND US

Long after bones have turned to dust, and civilizations to history, it is the sorcery of the past which continually endures. Before antiquarians took an interest in 'rude heathen stone circles', the local communities associated these locations with rich fairy folklore and healing traditions. The sorcery endured within the consciousness of the folk spirit—by being directly connected to the stone megaliths—while all else had long decayed. The spells of the ancient past still enchant us to this day. We may have fragments of pottery and arrowheads from the Neolithic era. However, few stop to think that the most resilient artifact from ancient times is the *Will* of these people. Or, at least, the *Will* of their shamans and wizards. John Foster Forbes was also the proponent of a most interesting theory; in that the original builders of the megaliths became caught up in a dark occult religion, and this 'sorcery' is what unleashed the disaster which led to the destruction of Atlantis. Following this, a new school of 'druids' arrived with the intention of restoring the 'path of light' to the stone circles and dolmens. Their efforts helped to stabilize this reality and end the psychic and social turmoil. Yet, the damage had already been done. Forbes also warned that dark occult forces of the present era are still attempting to corrupt the megaliths of Europe towards their own ends.

In his book, *The Castle and Place of Rothiemay*, Forbes recalls a childhood experience, when an influential friend of his father generated something of a psychic attack upon the young Forbes. The aristocrat joked about human sacrifices of young boys at a nearby Neolithic stone circle. Forbes makes it clear to the reader that his childhood instincts were telling him this aristocratic gentleman was not lying about sacrificing children continuing at certain ancient sites. The young Forbes had good reason to be concerned. For me personally, my favorite, and highly intriguing J. J. Foster Forbes theory is that of something of a 'literal Freemasonry'—"MARK THE TERM!" as Forbes wrote—which puts forward the idea that it is the nature of dry stone construction which allows megalithic structures to survive for millennia. That, rather than these stones just being randomly piled one upon the other, each stone within a megalithic structure—no matter how small or irregular—belongs in a very specific place. Its location within the dry stone wall is determined by the subconscious awareness of the builder. This is what makes the structure sacred and why later Christian churches were built upon them.

Forbes cited the example of dry stone walls used in field boundaries, and their ability to stand intact for hundreds of years due to the farmer carefully choosing specific stones for certain points in the wall. A symbiotic relationship between farmer and a particular stone—in a pile of perhaps hundreds—that calls out to be placed in a very specific location. Forbes also believed that masonry held by cement mortar was always doomed to fall apart, and constantly needed repairs. However, dry or loose stones developed a relationship with one another—like the sympathetic resonance of musical notes—because their placement in the structure was determined by direct subconscious communication with the builder. The farmer or wall builder is not merely building a dry stone wall, but constructing something of a magical boundary. These relationships are fine-tuned to not only last thousands of years—as free-standing stone structures—but also, loose stones transmit psychometric information to people who can read the messages contained within the stones. As long as the structures remain intact. That being, stones contain the memories of the events they witnessed and certain sensitive humans can access this archive.

ROCKS OF AGES

Although it is well known that the megalithic cultures of western and southern Europe placed great spiritual and healing significance upon particular stones—as well as megaliths formed from these special stones—this belief in the supernatural abilities of stone did not die out with the Christianized tribes of the 'lost' European megalithic civilizations. The sheer number of churches built—and also incorporating former sacred Pagan stones into their structures—upon pre-Christian ritual sites is proof enough of a continuation/co-option of this magical belief.

In regions of Portugal (such as Monsanto), massive boulders—which all had/have great Pagan spiritual and supernatural significance—have actual church buildings and other structures grafted on to them. Often in the most bizarre and enchanting methods of unorthodox architectural juxtapositions. As mentioned in my book, *The Druid Code: Magic, Megaliths and Mythology*, these magical properties are generally associated with the presence of quartz within these sacred stones. The connection between sorcery and sacred stones can also be found in Ireland among such traditions as the *Cursing Stones*; a table-like stone in which round, grapefruit-sized boulders are ritually rotated to cast or repel curses. *Bargaining Stones* are another type of magical stone tradition— surviving into the present—that have a hole through them in which oaths are taken by both parties joining hands through the hole. There is also the fascinating *Bullaun Stones*, used to collect rainwater for healing properties.

Among the Slavic nations—and within Slavic sorcery and folklore—the traditional Pagan magical properties of stone were appropriated within several Christian reinterpretations. Sacred stones being compared to the magical crystals upon the breastplate of the High Priest in *Exodus*. Slavic sacred stones are also compared to the magical foundation stones of the *Heavenly City*, as described within the *Book of Revelations*. Although these associations are towards Hebrew texts, the origin of these tales is almost certainly rooted within early Canaanite Pagan tradition. Such ideas of stones having a magical nature within the Christian bible would not have been lost on early Christians in the former Celtic, Slavic and Germanic pagan worlds. This is the only reason why early Christian churches were built upon stone Pagan temples and other sacred sites. By the Middle Ages, the same underlying sanctity and power of stone was adopted and re-imagined by the alchemists who chose the concept of stone as being the essential transformative symbol of both material and spiritual matters. *The Philosopher's Stone*. In this sense, the alchemists were not entirely dissimilar from the early shamans (and later druids) of the Celtic and megalithic European arc, by paying homage to the exceptional qualities of certain stones.

Sacred and magical stones also allowed—or symbolized—a transformation of states of consciousness, along with numerous healing abilities, such as babies being passed through holes in sacred stones. As well as ornamental stones and stonework being used at locations considered to be entrances to the Inner Earth. This includes the very magical and ritualistic Oweynagat Cave in Ireland (considered the 'mouth of hell' by the Christians), as well as the truly spectacular subterranean ritualistic landscape of the *Hypogeum of Hal-Saflieni* in Malta. By the Elizabethan age, the work of John Dee, in particular, generated a great re-interest in the magical properties of stone. The powerful traveling magicians and witches of Finland—during this same era—were considered something akin to superstars of European magical and occultic sciences, and were consulted by the highest levels of royalty and government for their divination and magical protective skills. Venerating the *Cult of Ukko* (another thunder/sky god), these Finnish magicians advised Ivan the Terrible to place magical stones within his staff. Once again, demonstrating how seriously magic and sorcery is taken, and always central to royalty and the aristocratic classes. In Britain, the *Stone of Scone* or the *Stone of Destiny*, has been used for centuries during the coronations of the kings of Scotland, and later, the monarchs of England and the Kingdom of Great Britain. The last time this took place was in 1953, with the coronation of Elizabeth II. The *Stone of Scone* will almost certainly be utilized for its magical properties by the coronation of the next British monarch. The BBC and other mass media covering the events will pass this off as being a 'great tradition', while never actually explaining why the *Stone of Scone* is actually involved in coronations to begin with. The higher you go up the social ladder, one finds that magic and sorcery are everywhere.

Veneration of the magical properties and symbolism of stone has also resulted in some appalling acts of very real pathological sorcery performed during the construction of important stone structures in the past. For hundreds of years—and under the jurisdiction of the Christian authorities—it was not uncommon to bury alive a new born baby within the walls of a newly constructed bridge or city wall. A very real human sacrifice, in order to give the structure the soul of the child, so the building would very literally be alive. Over the centuries, renovations upon numerous old buildings and infrastructure in German cities has led to the discovery of small coffins with the bones of infants contained inside. In one case, over a hundred baby coffins were found during renovations of Bremen's city walls in 1589. The famous *Lia Fáil* stone upon the sacred Hill of Tara in Ireland—purported to have been brought to Ireland by the ancient magical race known as the Tuatha Dé Danann—was moved and placed upon the mass grave of thousands of Irish rebels who had been taken prisoner and disemboweled and left to die there following a battle in 1798. Someone involved in that process knew precisely what they were doing in moving the *Lia Fáil* by placing it above a grave of mass sacrificial victims. Blood sorcery and stone. The relocation of the sacred stone was the culmination of a ritual. These rituals still go on—in a 'metaphorical' sense—with many Freemasonic organizations who 'charge' the cornerstone of new constructions with the 'symbolic' flesh and blood of a child using animal fat and wine. Such practices serve as an example of how sorcery and magical ritual—in the wrong hands—can eventually deteriorate into horrors.

THE MAGICAL PROTECTIVE PROPERTIES OF QUARTZ

One of the first and most important acts we can personally perform—as part of our magical and spiritual self-development—is to incorporate quartz into our lifestyle. To protect our homes and ourselves from unwarranted non-material pathological forces and energies. A large piece of white snow quartz on our bedside table can help us sleep better at night. This will enhance the quality, and thereby, the usefulness of our dreaming as a means of effective communication with our subconscious minds. This will also help to deflect psychic attacks from malevolent individuals and entities, as well as provide us with an object of great beauty to admire. I would suggest we take a very traditional *Folk Magic* approach to procuring the white quartz, and look for some naturally occurring samples. Rocky mountain regions as well as beaches are the best locations to find the stone. Often, the right piece of white quartz will find you. I myself found—during a mountain hike—a beautiful piece of snow quartz shaped similar to, and about the same size as, a human heart. It has provided me with excellent energetic protection and charge over the years.

Pondering the simulacra contained within the rock's features creates a bond between you and the stone, in much the same way that the images and symbols of a specific *Tarot* card become our personal charged narrative over time. To increase the charge of the snow quartz, place it under the glow of the full moon—if the sky is clear—and occasionally allow rainwater to wash over it. Protect and safeguard this piece of quartz, and it will return this respect in kind. Building some form of decorative plinth or mount for the quartz to sit upon also enhances its beauty and presentation. Venerate the beauty and properties of the quartz and it will reward you for it. Charge this psychic battery with your intention and *Will*.

GNOSIS AND DEMONS

In many ways, we experience reality—in its present form—by means of quantum-based and psychological generation of matter and experience through specific use of words, phrases and language. What you speak is what you generate. Very few people are aware of just how powerful and potentially risky usage of language can be. Further to this, our personal relationship with the fabric of existence—both internal and external—is based, to a large degree, on forces and experiences created by the use of specifically structured language and particular sounds.

While the subconscious mind itself functions within a lexicon of symbols —and communicates to our conscious minds through the medium of metaphors, dreams and artistic exploration—it is words and language that brings the unconscious into manifestation. This is the 'action' of language. After all, this is central to the cognition we have devised in order to 'navigate' the reality we manifested for ourselves. Think of your subconscious as being the rocket that propels you into space, language being the spacesuit that keeps you alive while in space. Within the domain of ritual, ceremonial magic and sorcery, certain words and phrases have a specific power force contained within them, via their time-embellished mystique, and also by their actual verbal utterance. These words and phrases can allow something of a group call to take place between the lower poles of cognition, the conscious mind, and the nature of the reality surrounding us. The specific use of a word or phrase —along with how it is stated—can literally soften the material fabric of reality, and can open up something of a portal between the cosmic and the subconscious.

These terms and chants do not so much 'hack' the operating system of the universe, per se. It is more a case that they allow us to access the underlying code-generating reality. Granted, this is a rather crude metaphor, but a metaphor useful in understanding the limitations and potentials involved. Sometimes we can rewrite this code, and sometimes we cannot.

However, the repetitive use of the terms and chants eventually begins to loosen the sub-atomic field surrounding us, and this can allow the possibility of altering or changing present and future circumstances. Hence, the universal reliance upon incantation within ritual and rites. In the beginning was the word.

ABRACADABRA

The incantation of *Abracadabra* has been used for thousands of years in order to increase the energetic forces of the human body and mind, so as to aid in everything from fighting disease to energizing the pure streams of energy required for magical spells and rituals. The unknown antiquity of the phrase suggests that it was derived from the deep primal past of human history. It may even have been one of the first complex, multi-syllable terms or phrases uttered by humans who moved beyond the creation and adoration of petroglyphs and rock art of our most distant ancestors. Although the phrase is most generally attributed to having its origins in the Aramaic tongue, this remains a hotly contested theory. Its historical mystery only attests to the antiquity—if not the universality—of the power of reciting the incantation of "*Abracadabra*" aloud. What we can verify about its origins is that the phrase has been considered extremely powerful across history and in many cultures. In Hebrew, it translates as "I create like the word." Again, to convey the links between the mind, language and the formation of relative materialism.

This manner of phraseology is also common across many Indo-European linguistic traditions, and generally rests upon the same idea of 'what you speak is what you create'. In more esoteric terms, the use of the phrase *Abracadabra* almost certainly increases the auric state around a person. This is something of an energetic advantage, and allows the proficient magician to create a level of plasticity within the *Quantum* field around them. Please note that when I use terms such as *Quantum, Dark Matter/Energy, Matrix* and so on, these are simply the 'terms du jour', so to speak, in order to convey the underlying and unseen mysterious dynamics of the universe. In years to come, science will no doubt invent new terms for these underlying and mysterious events and experiences. Mythology does this all the time, which is what makes mythology so relevant. From demons to gray aliens, only the cultural branding has changed. The underlying phenomenon remains constant.

The aforementioned *Cunning Folk* of London and other English cities would paint *Abracadabra* on the doors of houses during a plague, or other epidemic outbreak, as the threshold to a home was considered to be something of an energetic barrier against pathological forces—both seen and unseen—and, by extension, the spiritual security of those residing within. This depends upon how this 'portal' was given protection or lack thereof. Anyone reading this book—and who is serious about embarking upon a magical exploration—will have to develop a new relationship with their own living space if they are to remain safe from unwanted intrusions. You are opening a very big door.

SPIRITUAL HYGIENE

Apotropaic Magic represented in objects and symbols, such as the almost universal *Hamsa,* or *Khams*—all come from a time when a house or home was considered very much as a sacred space requiring great protection from unwarranted forces and individuals. A precaution that many people today would do well to take themselves in these times when homes are made fully accessible to complete strangers, along with any possible entities and forces which they may be carrying along with them. Often, the bearer of these forces has no malicious intentions towards the occupants of the home they are visiting. The mentally ill, alcoholics and drug addicts can unknowingly carry in and unleash negative forces and entities into a home that they are visiting.

Quarantine does not start only and end with germs and viruses. Today, we can place small items, to act as *Talismans,* upon the front door frame on the exterior doorstep. Which is why *Abracadabra* painted on doors—during times of mass plague outbreak—was taken very seriously. This is not to say we nail shut our front doors and live as recluses from society, but we still must take precautions. When we develop our *charisma* by embarking upon the acceptance and study of magic and sorcery, we can sometimes find that we become a kind of a psychic food source for the nonself-generating types who live in society. The *Meat Golems,* as I call them. As I have pointed out in my work dealing with psychopathic individuals, these types tend to target gifted, unique people and their psychic and sexual life energies. What certain types of persons can't create for themselves, they will attempt to harvest off others. This is why we protect ourselves with *Apotropaic Magic.* Hence, why we need *Talismans* on the thresholds of our homes to ward them off.

The Jewish *Mezuzah is* an excellent example of this. However, all cultures have their own versions of this protective totem. In old Ireland, mothers would religiously wash the doorstep of the front of their houses for the same reason. Even door knockers resplendent with the heads of lions and other dangerous animals, are all rooted in an ancient desire to ward off the *Evil Eye* of the pathological intruder.

DARKENED CORNERS

A common *Folk Magic* belief in much of Europe—which arrived by means of Sumerian demonology—was the idea that demons and other malevolent entities 'nest' within the mildew and mold that often accumulates in the damp corners of old dwellings. By regular cleaning and painting of these musty demonic nesting points, a home can be kept free of 'evil' beings residing among the mold and fungus. While there is clearly an obvious metaphor here pertaining to the 'demons' actually being airborne fungal infections, it is also worth noting that until the Roman Empire, Europeans lived almost exclusively in circular dwellings. If the buildings were 'long house' type structures, often the corners would be 'rounded off' somehow, with upright poles set into them, or the plaster rendering was curved around so as to make one straight wall merge into the other without hard corners. Superstition is often culturally-generated sorcery with surprisingly practical outcomes if one is inclined towards rationalizing such ideas.

Some magicians even allow their living spaces to purposely deteriorate, with the intention of making a location more desirable for entities to come and live among the sorcerer. Certainly this appears to have been the case with Austin Osman Spare, who, towards the end of his life, was reported to be living among demons in a home he never kept clean. No great artist ever had an immaculate studio. This also adds weight to the notion of rundown and ruined, large buildings such as abandoned hospitals, mine shafts, prisons and asylums being hot spots of paranormal and demonic activity. Cornish tin miners, for example, took entities such as the *Piskey folk* and the *Knocker* very seriously. It is hardly surprising to also note that most stately homes generally become 'haunted' when their financial upkeep begins to dwindle.

PROTECTING THE SACRED SPACE

We live in an age whereby most people are ignorant and dismissive of spiritual hygiene. This is a most unfortunate state of affairs, as a person's presence within their home should be treated with all the sanctity that bees apply to their hive. Which is why the alchemists used the symbolism of the bee hive to represent the ideal temperature of the human soul. A healthy bee hive interior and a healthy human body generate almost identical temperatures.

Have you ever been inside a home or house that seemed to require less heat than other houses in order to be warm and comfortable in winter, no matter how old it was? Conversely, have you ever entered a house that always seemed cold, regardless of how well made, how well heated and insulated it was? This effect is directly related to the spiritual hygiene of the environment. Coldness, for no apparent reason, is an energetic dissipation out of the localized environment, and can be an indication of an entity or psychic vampire living there. Spiritual activity can also be indicated by mysterious pools of water appearing for no apparent reason, although this is not generally worrisome, as such. Even so, we should take notice of these 'leaks'. If a plumber or roofer can't solve them, the source is usually of a non-material origin. Often, repainting the room—as well as rearranging the furniture—can be enough to move these forces 'on', so to speak. To begin tending to one's spiritual hygiene, I have found that regular recital of, as well as making and displaying *Talismans* containing the phrase *Abracadabra* offers remarkable spiritual and psychic protection within one's home. So I would suggest that you incorporate the term into your own life. Especially if you decide to embark on a very specific magical practice after reading this book.

Aleister Crowley himself held the power of the phrase in high esteem, although he changed it slightly, to '*Abrahadabra*', by changing the 'c' to a 'h' within his *Book of the Law* (1904), citing that 'h' represented the *Breath of Life,* as well as the Egyptian god Horus. While thousands of Thelemites have been perfectly contented to use the phrase in the manner in which Crowley rephrased it, this adaptation also serves to demonstrate the often overlooked adaptability and improvisation (within certain limitations) of magical practice and rituals. Like all art forms, sorcery can have powerful soloists and free-form virtuoso performers. Once the underlying intention is honest, and 'from the heart', so to speak. However, the undoubted power of the term *Abracadabra* lies in the methodology of its use in terms of how it is said and altered (compressed) within a very specific incantation. Within the magical tradition, "*Abracadabra*" is recited nine times in order to deflect negative forces or entities—while placing us in a somewhat magical state—beginning with the full word and ending with the 'a' sound, which is pronounced as 'ah'. After this, the incantation is then reversed, and, beginning with the 'a', returning in stages to the completed "*Abracadabra*" once again.

SALUTATION OF THE RISING SUN

A highly effective form of using this phrase is to perform it each morning according to the cardinal points of North, South, East and West. Beginning in the East, and moving to the West, the North and then finally, the South. There are some regional variations of this movement. I am basing the order of salutation as performed by Irish *Fairy Doctors*—a kind of Gaelic shaman once very popular in rural Ireland—during their own specific coordinated incantations, although they would have most likely used incantations specific to Irish gods and goddesses, such as Brid. However, **always begin facing to the East**, regardless of how you perform the rest of the process. This ritual is especially effective in charging the internal magical state. It is a very useful exercise for people who have no previous experience in sorcery. If there is an East-facing window in the home—so as to face the rising sun to begin the incantation —all the better. In old rural Ireland, the main entrances of houses always faced East for this reason, as this orientation went back to the very ancient veneration of the rising sun. Write the stages of the *Abracadabra* incantation on a sheet of paper and read from it until you are able to recite it by heart.

The preceding graphic demonstrates how performing the ritual in this manner creates the shape of the *Maltese Cross* or the *Cross Pattée*; *a* symbol long associated with healing and power, and later adopted among organizations such as the *Knights Hospitaller* and the *Order of Saint John*. The design is not a Christian symbol in origin. It can even be found at ancient druid sites. The symbol of the *Maltese Cross* is strongly connected to the universal and ancient magical symbols of the *Sun Cross* and the *Swastika*. All are ultimately associated with salutation towards the Sun and its solar, life-giving and regenerative powers.

The invocation of solar deities and archetypes is central to morning magical incantations, regardless of the deity being either Horus or Lugh, or any other god or goddess. The ritual is the charging of our own star— within ourselves—by aligning it with the star at the center of our energetic solar system. The daily salutation of the rising Sun becomes something of a microcosmic symbol of the initial creation of the universe itself. However, it is the magician who is creating his or her own microcosmic universe.

HECATE

MAGICAL GODDESS OF CROSSROADS AND THRESHOLDS

The incredibly powerful Ancient Greek goddess of Magic is Hecate (Hekate). Seen here in her Hellenic triple form. She is the protector of crossroads, door-ways, light, gives wisdom of natural herbs and poisonous plants, ghosts, necromancy, and sorcery. The power of her archetype has spread even into Catholic nations, in the form of the Virgin Mary, where her icon can be found at remote rural crossroads inside a glass shrine. Especially in rural Ireland, Sicily and Iberia.

CHAOS, THE MODERN FOLK MAGIC

As with any good Pagan, the visible world—to me—is a very spiritual experience in the fullest sense. This includes all the experiences of this consciousness-generated extravaganza, both joyous and tormenting. Every facet of existence is made up of the necessary components in order to create a circuit board of our material world. Within *Chaos Magic* practice, the aim is to allow these forces to move and flow through the magician. Then accepting—if not cherishing—all and every outcome as useful and meaningful to one degree or another. These ideas were central to a group known as the highly satirical *Discordian Society,* who venerated Eris, the Greek goddess Chaos, proving that you can't keep a good Pagan archetype down.

This ability to move and flow with shifts and changes in the world can also been seen as using the turbulent paradigm of the times in order to kick off the cobwebs (spiritual hygiene again) of conformist safety in order to generate the new modality of intellect and creativity, so as to make us become more effectively potentialized as individuals. The creation of the best possible version of you. The person you were meant to be, and not what society expected you to be.

We live in an age whereby people are too quick to feel victimized by some political idea, or pundit making a statement, which they feel personally offended by. Usually, for highly subjective and conditioned reasons, generally known only to the 'victim' who is merely carrying the baggage of some cultural or political dogma handed to them from some external influence. By assuming such a reaction, they have effectively chained themselves to a kind of co-dependency bondage with their object of hate. This is very much a kind of pathological entanglement, and one which serves no meaningful spiritual or psychological outcome. Further to this, the politician or media figure they have deluded themselves into believing they are being tormented by is actually being fed by the life force of the self-generated victim.

Because the 'offense' was not personally directed at the 'offended', the stream of energetic charge is directed one-way only: towards the politician or entity they hate. This only feeds and empowers the politician, media figure or entity which they are constantly hating. The results of wasting one's energy in this manner can be somewhat devastating for the 'offended' individual. Everything from insanity and/or poor health and even self-mutilation. While the politician or pundit they hate goes on to even greater levels of power and influence. Don't tell me you haven't seen someone you know literally self-hexing themselves with this very scenario. This is a form of magic many people have seen in their own lives. Look at the alcoholism, cancer rates and divorce figures among tabloid journalists, for example. Attacking people who have done you no personal harm comes with a heavy energetic toll. Within proficient use of modern magic and sorcery, the idea is to not care; or, at most, satirize the politician or pundit. This prevents one's energy from being fed to them.

Rather than believing some shadowy cabal controls the planet, assume that no one is in charge. The irony of which is that you become in charge of your own destiny. You become the ruler of your own world. This is the kind of *Tactical Sorcery* which one can garnish from *Chaos Magic* and use it to great effect within one's own life. The writings of Robert Anton Wilson were highly inspirational to the early architects of *Chaos Magic*, in that complex, studious ritual, as well as the occultic self-importance of past traditions of ceremonial sorcery—now in the era of *Quantum Physics*—were actually becoming barriers to effective manifestation of magical intention. The Victorian-inspired snobbery and elitism of groups such as the *Golden Dawn* were problematic when it came to the effective outcome of the *Will* in a world of advancing technology and rapid cultural expansion. Rather, *Chaos* magicians took inspiration from popular culture, such as the writings of Michael Moorcock, Philip K. Dick, H.P. Lovecraft's *Cthulhu Mythos*, and meshed these inspirations into the emerging popularity of *Quantum Theory*, *Punk Rock* and the *Chaos Science* of late 1970s. All of this was eventually bonded into *Chaos Magic*, when Peter J. Carroll and Ray Sherwin proposed (correctly) their theory that the very act of belief itself was a power source. This was a truly monumental development in the history of sorcery and the occult. A quantum leap that effectively transformed *Ceremonial Magic* into something of a lifestyle instead. One did not just perform magic. One was magic.

THE SORCERY OF THE SELF

Remember what I wrote in the first chapter, about energy being neutral at the point of zero? Once we move from that point of neutrality—in either direction—the charge of magical potential is in full effect. The start of the ritual is no more inert than the completion of the ritual. This is why a ritual begun and left uncompleted can have very real—and sometimes dire—consequences. Don't start what you can't finish. Many know how to "Open Sesame". However, not many consider that they also have to close it.

With *Chaos Magic*, the ritual is essentially on-going within the secret life of the magician. Observant—while emotionally detached—as the psyche moves among the unfolding dynamic of the social and cultural changes around them. Ostensibly, this is a modern re-engineering of the *Folk Magic* of our ancestors. Ancestors who had *Charms*, *Talismans*, spells, invocations, blessings during the preparation of food, as well as cures for just about everything. Everything in their lives had a magical thread woven through it. All cultures on this planet have these rituals except modern Western culture. They were taken from us deliberately, so they could be sold back to us in high-profitable repackaging.

There is no reason why our modern lives should not also be infused with the same sense of sacred existence. Every mundane and ordinary event and aspect can then take on the most profound meaning. Wisdom can pour forth from what you once considered the banalities of life. This baseline of your constant awareness of occasional coincidences, synchronicity and simulacra manifesting around you gently amplifies your overall magical state. The star within you glows with a constant, elevated luminescence.

Less things will go wrong in your life. You will begin to see the pain of your past as the heroic challenges—which you overcame—and not the root of any victimhood. The world becomes filled with creative tools and opportunities. You will meet the people you need to meet. Simply by removing, satirizing or seeking deeper meanings within the unfolding dynamics of the world around us, we remove the buffers. The social and cultural dynamic then becomes a power force of the age. A power force that flows through you, along with the vast levels of psychic energy you will have retained for your own journey to godhood.

STAR MAN AND DRAG QUEENS

Our life will become something of an unending ritual. Consider the career of David Bowie—from *Ziggy Stardust* to *Blackstar*—as an example within the context of a popular cultural icon. *Major Tom, Aladdin Sane* and *The Jean Genie* were all shamanic expressions of his craft. *Drag Queens* are, likewise, also a kind of modern shaman. This is why, upon encountering a *Drag Queen* for the first time, we are often overwhelmed with a sense of magical explosiveness which they present us with.

Drag Queen acts were very popular among working class males when I was growing up in Dublin. The reason being that the genetic memory of these tough heterosexual males were subconsciously recognizing the *Drag Queen* as being the shaman of the modern age. It is also interesting that many of the famous and most popular *Drag Queens* in the UK and Ireland were Irish or of Irish heritage, such as Danny La Rue, Mr. Pussy and Lily Savage. Perhaps their own ancestors were the shamans who stood upon the cyclopean stones of Stonehenge and other ancient stone temples. Who can forget the sheer magical intensity of the scene in the Australian movie *The Adventures of Priscilla, Queen of the Desert,* in which the three drag queens overlook a sacred Aboriginal site within *Watarrka National Park* while dressed in the most outrageous costumes. Magic is simply everywhere once you begin to stop resisting the conventions of everyday society and observe the ordinary with visionary eyes. All of us—as individuals—can also incorporate these new forms of shamanism within our own day-to-day lives.

You do not have to be visually or behaviorally exceptional—in public—in order to reach such states, either. Your charisma, your rules. Behind closed doors—in the privacy of your own home—you can transform yourself into any manner of jester, magician or shaman you wish to be. Once you are not hurting another person, and are within the magic circle of your own home, you are no longer a conformist prisoner of the social conventions beyond the threshold. This is the awesome power of secrecy and seclusion once more. No one is ever depressed while playing A*ir Guitar* to their favorite record, alone at home. In this sense, the entire concept of social respectability and 'correct' behavior can be seen in terms of a *Black Magic* operation imposed upon us. So as to nullify our natural shamanic inclinations. That 'correct' knife and fork spell once more...

During the early days of *Chaos Magic,* the resurgence of *Psychonautics* —that being, exploring states of human consciousness through newer forms of shamanism and ritual—exploded out from Carroll's and

Sherwin's initial meetings and became something of an influential cultural—and even technological—*tour de force* by the 1990s, inspiring not only a new generation of young occultists, but also movie makers, artists, computer software/gaming developers, as well as comic book artists and writers. This 'street-wise sorcery' approach avoids the overly academically-inclined resistance—which most people have come to view as barriers—towards incorporating new paradigms and cultural changes into their personal lives as well as magical practice.

NOT WASTING ONE'S MAGICAL POWER

Archaic sorcery that resists the unfolding complexity of new and emerging paradigms eventually leads to stagnation. Inertia is experienced by both the society and the individuals resisting these new complexities and dynamic nuances which are constantly bubbling up from the collective unconsciousness. In many ways, H.P. Lovecraft's Cthulhu— rising from the depths of the subconscious mind, as well as the depths of the oceans—can be seen as the psychological monster created by an inability of individuals to deal with the changing complexities of the society around them.

By not being tormented by social and cultural changes, but instead, approaching these events with neutral and detached consideration, one will not be torn asunder by them in the misguided belief that they can be stopped. In this light, Cthulhu can be seen as something of a literary

Daemon of Lovecraft's own difficult relationship with modernity. The lesson here for the magician is to not waste the light of your inner magical star by attempting to diminish what you can't directly change by means of the blinding haze of your own revulsion. Protect your psychic energy as you would your sacred spaces. By allowing them to flow freely within and around us, we avoid the trauma and stress of any paralyzing conservatism or obsolete mindset. This, then, allows our own psychic and creative energy to be more effectively retained and used for ourselves— and our loved ones—in a more useful and productive manner. This ability to ride the moving and chaotic high-speed paradigms of this modern *Internet* age is ostensibly the folk wisdom of the times. This is what made *Chaos Magic* so incredibly liberating and exciting when it first entered into the occultic tradition. Boiling down personal experience into the most effective magical attributes possible, and creating one's own personal system of sorcery, it is effectively bringing *Folk Magic* back to the people. Ultimately, there is little difference between the personal magical beliefs and practices generated by an advertising accounts manager in New York than that of a rural witch in 17th century Iberia who had developed her own craft and spells. The proof is ultimately in the pudding. The end results will be self-evident, or not at all.

The *Chaos* magician's power is in that he or she is not overtly a self-conscious magi or priestess. They are, rather, the ordinary man and woman in the street in how they appear to the rest of society. However, they are using very basic, accessible forces and powers to enhance their own quality of life, to deal more effectively with modern social challenges as they arise. What worked for Aleister Crowley in late 1910 —when he performed the remarkable *Rites of Eleusis* ritual at Caxton Hall, London—can't be directly transferred into a modern office space or contemporary suburban street. Deconstruction and compression of these traditional magical rituals and forces are how we make them useful in today's society.

DYNAMIC GNOSIS

As society and culture changes with such rapid pace, psychic and creative energy is as abundant to us today as the forces of the natural world were to previous generations of witches, druids and shamans. It is just the format of the energy, and how it is contained, that is different. However, it still remains the same exploitable resource for the fertilization of our consciousness and the enhancement of our mystical lives. This is what makes the *Sigil* such a powerful force of our age. Corporations and governments were quick to recognize this potential of these 'logos' early on in the 20th century. In the past, one could invoke the gods of the forests and mountains; however, while these gods and goddesses still exist—and can still be called upon—they are out of the reach of people living within our modern urban areas and concrete metropolitan jungles. Instead, we must seek *Valhalla* in the shopping malls, and *Mount Olympus* on the commuter train. So rather than call upon the demons and spirits of the wild places, we become living gods ourselves and refrain from subscribing our emotional richness towards political, social and other cultural ideas of association and conformity. As I have already stated, magicians are the ultimate anarchists. What gives *Chaos Magic* its prime potential is the tactical aspect of looking and observing the swirling dynamic of the unfolding turmoil around us, and not allowing it to imprison us within its restricting *milieu*. Our feral psychic energy in such environments can be tremendously liberating. It creates magical opportunities for personal self-growth and vitality of life enhancements by the mere act of not being energetically drained by the fast-moving paradigm shifts of the present age. Instead, we are allowed to claim salvage rights from the wreckage of cultural and social tropes unfolding, evolving—and destroying themselves—all around us. For me personally, this was the most liberating aspect of *Chaos Magic*. It allowed me to improvise and use all the tools at my disposal in creative and very exciting ways.

SELF-MADE AND SELF-CREATED GODS

This is not to say that the old rules and rituals are to be thrown away. Not at all. They become components, modified and personalized. *Tarot* cards, art, ancient rites, sacred landscapes, simulacra, along with a fertile imagination, are all generating dynamic, bespoke mystical processes and states. Our magical *charisma* is far more attainable than religion has previously made us assume. One person's blasphemy is another person's liberation. Every familiar god and goddess represents localized archetypes—as components of the whole—broken down into specific forces of nature and aspects of the psyche. By naming these gods according to our specific cultures, it allows a greater focus upon these archetypal attributes. Then, through this specific identification, we can influence—and be influenced by them—to a more highly specific degree.

For example, a period of strife in your life can be connected to a god—or heroic mythological figure—who has also endured hardship, and who has eventually triumphed over adversity. By doing so, you are projecting your psychic state towards the successful outcome, rather than being trapped within the hopeless despondency of the moment. You will then find that the solutions to problems and challenges begin resolving themselves unexpectedly before you. Heroes and wizards will arrive to help you. You 'have gotten out of the way of yourself' by becoming more than just yourself. This new 'space' you have created eventually becomes filled with what you need.

Identifying spiritual beings by their names and attributes, we are more able to consider ourselves to be spiritual beings. We are invoking their higher power within us. This simple act slowly chips away at the frontiers of five-sense limitations. However, we can also create—and adapt—our own gods and goddesses, too. In popular culture—from comic book heroes to TV and movie characters—this happens all the time. This is why Joseph Campbell placed as much importance on the archetype of Luke Skywalker as he did King Arthur. Pick or create your own archetype and run with it.

GNOSIS

Key to this accessibility of magical states and potentials is the idea of *Gnosis*. The term is derived from a Greek concept of 'knowledge' (in the broadest and metaphysical sense) reaching or attaining states of awareness and enlightenment. It is the psychic self-generation of the 'divine spark' connecting with the underlying intelligence of the cosmos. What makes this idea so powerful is that this is essentially a self-carved path, outside the jurisdictions of any religion or dogma. It was precisely this sense of spiritual/mystical self-internalization which led to the followers of Gnosticism to be brutally persecuted by the early Christian churches. Especially in Egypt, as it was seen as a back door towards Paganism, and in particular, *Classical* occultism.

Today, the ideas of *Gnosis* are generally looked upon as being associated with spiritual or magical self-development by means of altered states of consciousness, and can be interpreted as being the Western version of the Buddhist concept of *Samadhi*. The mind—while silent—is deeply focused within the present moment, and this lends itself perfectly to the practice of sorcery. Hence, why *Samadhi* appealed to both Crowley and Austin Osman Spare. It allows a transition from the traditional invocations of directly contacting spirits and demons as enablers of magical powers, and, instead, presents the practitioner of magic with the ability to generate these forces from within himself or herself.

Rather than employing the archetypes for these purposes (although there is nothing at all wrong in doing this, as I do it myself constantly), the magical practitioner becomes the archetype(s), an extremely powerful process. The magician's thoughts are then targeted directly upon the outcome, and all other thoughts are removed in order to focus the *Will* completely upon this stream of psychic energy flowing through them. From this point on, the objective of the outcome is permanently sequestered within the subconscious mind. There are several methods of doing this, and all are equally effective. Once again, as with all sorcery, the method preferred is a personal choice.

INHIBITORY GNOSIS

An extremely deep form of waking meditation very similar to a self-induced hypnotic state, sensory deprivation is the most effective of the safe methods. Spending a period of time in a pitch black room, lost in an unfamiliar, isolated, rural location (especially at night), even an unknown urban location. Fasting. Not reading books. Not listening to music or watching TV for a specific period of time. At first, the mind goes into a sort of cognitive overdrive, filling itself with distractive thoughts and overly concerned observations, leading to all manner of mental confusion. However, this cognitive overdrive begins to stabilize eventually, and the conscious mind gives up. Our charge becomes neutral at the point of zero. Then the desires of the magician begin to operate within the subconscious mind. At this point, we begin to pour our concentration into what it is we wish to achieve, as if it has already come to pass.

ECSTATIC GNOSIS

This became very popular among *New Age Traveler* groups in the UK during the 1990s, who took an interest in the growing popularity of *Chaos Magic*, and it also supplemented the *Rave* culture of the same era. The idea is to generate total sensory overload through sexual orgasm, screaming, drumming, chanting offensive or disturbing phrases, self-induced near-suffocation (supervised, of course) and—during the Autumnal months in Europe—the use of *psilocybin* ('magic mushrooms'). The downside of being in the 'mosh pit', so to speak, of *Ecstatic Gnosis,* is that all the commotion may attract entities and pathological *Renfields* into a group setting. The risk of malicious and opportunistic individuals being drawn to such rituals—involving acts of sex and what some might consider hedonism—is a constant concern. I would advise against people drinking alcohol from partaking in this particular form of ritual. They do not call it 'spirits' and the 'demon drink' for nothing...

INDIFFERENT VACUITY

Another and very effective approach within *Gnosis*—from my own experience—is the concept of *Indifferent Vacuity,* which was developed by Phil Hine and Jan Fries. This is rooted in the idea that all thoughts ultimately derive from the collective consciousness, and have effectively already came to pass. What you desire has already happened at the moment you placed your *Will* upon it. So rather than a ritual or spell progressing the process along incremental stages of 1 through 10, the desire hits 10 instantly, so to speak. You will still have to implement the *Five Stages of Ritual Magic*. However, the psychological state of attained success becomes very powerful when incorporating *Indifferent Vacuity* into the process. It is akin to still having to walk up onto the stage to collect a prize you have already won.

Without applying *Indifferent Vacuity*, the complexity of our cognition and conscious awareness effectively functions as inhibitors or barriers to the manifestation of the desired outcome. Therefore, we need to 'get out of the way' of this process and allow the cosmos to handle the details. Key to this is to forget the initial intent of the ritual or *Sigil* and not to dwell on the outcome constantly—or at all if you can manage this—by allowing your conscious processes to stop impeding the spell or ritual and allowing it to do its thing. This is an extremely powerful process. If you are able to detach yourself successfully from the process, you will often have dreams of rivers flowing towards you. This is your subconscious mind informing you that the process is being managed independently of your attention being placed upon it. The most effective manner—for me personally—of applying *Indifferent Vacuity* is to put your mind towards a project or aspect of your life you wish to change, and then create a *Sigil* or *Five Stage Ritual* before this event. A good time to do this is right before you go on vacation, or embark upon a business venture or other real world project that will require your full attention. Your mind will be too occupied with day-to-day challenges and work schedules to be able to place any disruptive (interrupting) focus upon the outcome of the spell or *Sigil*. One can contemplate and analyze the spell, ritual or process **after** the desired outcome has come, or not come to pass. Even in the case of the spell failing, it is important to look at the whole process—from preparation to completion—and attempt to analyze where you may have went wrong. This is the science element of sorcery.

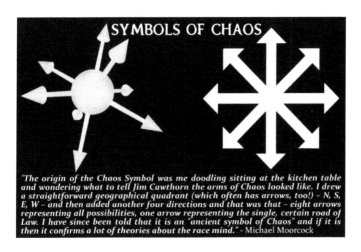

SYMBOLS OF CHAOS

"The origin of the Chaos Symbol was me doodling sitting at the kitchen table and wondering what to tell Jim Cawthorn the arms of Chaos looked like. I drew a straightforward geographical quadrant (which often has arrows, too!) – N, S, E, W – and then added another four directions and that was that – eight arrows representing all possibilities, one arrow representing the single, certain road of Law. I have since been told that it is an "ancient symbol of Chaos" and if it is then it confirms a lot of theories about the race mind." - Michael Moorcock

RENFIELD INTRUSIONS

In one particular case—while I was attempting to generate a magical process which involved the phases of the moon—the entire objective was thrown into turmoil by a certain type of individual I term as being a *'Renfield'*, after the insane human familiar of *Count Dracula* in the Bram Stoker novel. I was attempting to abstain from both alcoholic and solid food during certain phases of the lunar cycle in order to work towards a state of *Gnosis*, when this Renfielding individual—as a result of a demonic force working through his compromised psyche—unleashed the full intensity of his psychosis upon me. The ritual went completely wrong and fell apart, and, after a few days, was in tatters.

I had made the mistake of telling some people in private about my intention. Even though none of these people told anyone else, the verbal utterances of my *Will*—beyond my own cognition—put my desires out into the collective consciousness, so to speak. A particular individual I know—who is both psychotic and easily possessed by demonic entities as a result of an extreme case of alcoholism and cannabis addiction—basically went to war against me on social media for no apparent reason. Upon finding this out, it completely threw off my concentration and the ritual was wrecked. It was literally derailed by a 'walk-in' demon(s) using this *Renfield* as a ventriloquist would manipulate a dummy. This became an important lesson, in that never again would I tell anyone—not even close friends—when I was embarking upon a difficult and complex ritual. Once the objectives of my *Will* remained private—and I kept my mouth shut—it remained within my consciousness alone. I came to understand that the early successes of the ritual had made me somewhat boastful—or perhaps 'more excited' would be a proper reflection on the event—and my ego got in the way of the intended outcome. I blurted it out into the *aether*, and the wrong ears listened. This is an example of the science aspect of sorcery, in that I examined what went wrong and carefully refined my techniques accordingly.

ARE DEMONS ALWAYS WATCHING?

The manifestation or appearance of low-level entities can be very useful in gauging your growing powers of sorcery. Put it this way: when your magic begins to work, these entities notice, and, like moths to a flame, are drawn into the margins of your perception, where they can make their presence known by simple, and sometimes annoying, events. Books falling off shelves by themselves, objects moving, paintings and photos suddenly jumping off the nails or hooks—which they were securely hanging upon—are all very common signs that you have attracted attention.

In Indo-European cultures, these events were looked upon as fairies, goblins, sprites and other common spirits generally causing mischief. The reason why people today—even in rural areas—do not normally encounter these entities is not necessarily because they do not believe in them anymore. It is because magical ritual is no longer a part of everyday life within such communities to the level it once was. At a time when rural communities and households had rituals for just about everything, the magical charge of the environment was constantly heightened. Therefore, more entities were being drawn into this reality. When the rituals fell out of fashion, the entities had little to lure them into this reality to the level they once did. Therefore, even by the passive act of absorbing the information contained herein, you may have odd and puzzling events happen in your home: light bulbs exploding, electrical appliances failing, and mysterious pools of water appearing. Be aware, then, that you may have made yourself 'interesting' to these entities.

However, there is no cause for alarm, as they cannot, and have no desire to hurt you unless you purposely invoke more malevolent entities, or embark upon complex and intense ritual without mature and sound precautions. In such cases, the manifestation can be far more extreme; such as a large bird crashing into your window in full flight, or spontaneous fires igniting around you. I know one witch who had jars of jam and pickles exploding like grenades in her kitchen after she invited a friend over who offered her a *Ouija* board session. You are always given plenty of warning to move on to something else. If you are smart and you listen, that is. In most cases, such extreme manifestations are the exception and not the rule. Sometimes—and this can be most frightening to people—you will hear these entities speaking to you in archaic languages. These are the *Babblers in the Abyss,* usually whispering from inside your pillow when you are in bed at night, as well as within the hollow partitions of your interior walls, where they prefer the darkness. Again, this is a result of more intensive and on-going ceremonial rituals. When I first heard these demonic mutterings myself, I found the voices somewhat harrowing. This occurred when I was in college, and not until I understood the process properly—and what was actually happening—did I come to see that there was no direct danger, as such. They are spewing nonsense (babble) with the aim to traumatize you. Fear seems to feed them. Strange as it sounds, after a while, I actually felt empowered by the 'whispering demons'. It was a validation of my growing proficiency in the craft. I had opened a gate. Eventually, you do stop hearing them. Perhaps they become bored and move on. Again, take what you read in this book as far as you wish. Just do it with maturity and caution. You will find that what you once considered to be absurd and fanciful ends up staring you in the face when you are least expecting it. You are not going insane. You have blasted through the walls of reality.

As previously mentioned, the most common location to encounter entities and make them manifest—if this is your desire—are locations such as old abandoned hospitals, prisons and especially asylums. Such locations are also filled with magical charge as a result of the colossal psychic energy poured into their very structures by the purpose of their construction and use. Hence, why they are favorite locations for so-called *ghost hunters.*

Ancient stone circles and passage mounds at sacred sites are also magically charged from past ancient rituals having taken place within them. Many would say that, out of respect for the ancestors—in these particular places—do as the country folk of Ireland do, and leave well enough alone.

I have mixed feelings about this, as Christian churches have had no issue with tapping into the ancestral magic of such locations. So why not people like myself, who are more respectful of the craft of the druids and proto-shamanic sorcerers who ply their magical crafts at such places in the ancient past? Unlike religion, we are keeping the magical heritage of such stone circles and mounds alive. However, be warned. Far too many people make the mistake of assuming that all megalithic sites contain exclusively benign energies.

In 2015, at a very remote megalithic site in the mountains of Sardinia, I had been overcome with the desire to meditate inside one of the ancient stone chambers. Almost instantly, I knew I had been tricked. A powerful entity had attached itself onto me, and I spent next two nights in my hotel room in freezing cold baths of sea salt attempting to remove the presence. However, I was taught a very valuable lesson about impulse control at certain 'hot spots'. In the case of *ghost hunters*—inside an old hospital or railway tunnel—these paranormal investigators are (often) actually encountering demonic entities which have nested within these buildings.

They are not the trapped spirits of departed humans. While speaking at an event in Houston, Texas in 2017, I attempted to explain this to one well-known TV *ghost hunter,* and was met with with great surprise. He had never considered the possibility that these entities he was stalking and presenting on TV—with some considerable success—were actually demons and not ghosts. Who knows what whispering they do into the ears of the so-called *ghost hunters*—as these entities swarm around them, —unaware of what they are actually dealing with? After all, it was the nocturnal visitation of the "night gaunts" that whispered the *Cthulhu Mythos* into the ears of a young H.P. Lovecraft. Too often the hunter is actually the hunted. Know your limitations. Consider all and every possibility. Then work within them.

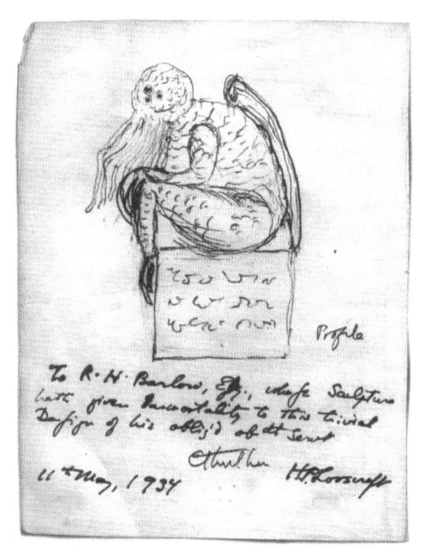

A sketch of Cthulhu, drawn by his creator, H.P. Lovecraft.

THE CHARGE AND THE CURSE

During my formative years, I had something of a nerdish obsession with electronics. A fascination with the harnessed electron. One which came directly out of a bizarre radio effect that took place in my early teens while listening to—and repeatedly turning the dial on—my AM transistor radio in the dark of the night. It is difficult these days to describe to people—in this age of digital broadcast—the imagination-meandering wonder of late-night electromagnetic globe-trotting across the AM dial, when all manner of broadcasts entered into one's head, as the metallic wand of the radio antenna grabbed a distant voice or song from out of the *aether*.

One night, while scanning the AM band for stations located all over Europe—and in a plethora of languages and accents—I suddenly heard an American voice saying "Rhode Island's largest Buick dealership..."

This was then followed by the music of an advertising jingle before the signal faded away into the myriad of radio waves arriving from Earth—and from outer space—into my transistor radio's germanium diode. The germanium diode itself, being a technology derived from the discovery of a crystal's rectifying abilities, was discovered by the German physicist and occultist Ferdinand Braun in 1874, who, incidentally, also demonstrated the first cathode ray tube oscilloscope. By guiding a narrow stream of electrons to a fluorescent screen inside a vacuum-sealed device known as a *Crookes Tube,* this became the first proper TV broadcast in history. For this event, Braun chose to project the ancient magical symbol which is known today as the *Maltese Cross.*

Amazingly, on the night in question—when I was being lobbied to momentarily consider an *'easy payment plan'* for something called a Buick—an AM radio transmission had somehow managed to travel three thousand miles across the Atlantic Ocean, eventually to be picked up by my plastic, red-colored, 9-volt battery-powered Phillips transistor radio located on the northside of Dublin, Ireland. Now while this was an incredible moment for me personally, it was hardly that unusual. Certain atmospheric and electromagnetic effects can indeed carry radio transmissions across vast distances. Some radio broadcasts have even come back from outer space—returning years later—only to be picked up by startled listeners. This is a form of time travel when you consider the idea more poetically, if not magically. What made this particular freak

AM signal reception so interesting was that, at the same time as the Rhode Island AM station made its way into my ear, there on my bedside table was a paperback copy of H.P. Lovecraft stories, which I had been enthusiastically working my way through at the time. The author himself was a product of the city of Providence, Rhode Island. It was almost as if my intense concentration had brought the radio signal across the vastness of the Atlantic Ocean. In fact—looking back on it now—this is precisely what had taken place. I was in such a state of intense hyper-awareness, coupled with deep imagination—along with intensive concentration and creativity—that the AM broadcast manifested within the compressed confines of the radio's ear piece.

From that point on, electronics—specifically pre-digital analog electronics—attained something of a magical dimension within my emerging teenage cognition. The combination of wires, resistors, capacitors, crystals and diodes—and what they could achieve by diverting streams of electrons into these components to be compressed into circuits—was very much a magical experience for me. I was also fully aware of the science and physics behind how all this worked. However, this did not make the experience any less magical for me. In fact, building a simple circuit and watching the glow of a red LED—or creating a radio transmitter of my own—only added to the very real 'magic' of the experience. Electronics was as near to *Alchemy* as I was going to get at that point in my life.

WHEN SCIENCE SUPPORTS SORCERY

Even though I was privy to the invisible mystery of how electromagnetism could travel across the empty space—between two coils by means of induction—it made the concept no less supernatural to me. The scientific theory and knowledge only served to copper-fasten my speculation that if electromagnetic forces can be transmitted across empty space, then why not human thoughts, life energy and so on? Further to this, could this effect be then converted into physical manifestations somewhere else? After all, the human body generates and transmits electromagnetic energy through its own nervous system. So why not also beyond ourselves?

The main issue within this line of speculation is that the human body—under normal circumstances—simply cannot transmit a large enough electromagnetic charge to move objects, or be able to communicate into another person's thoughts. Herein lies the crux of the matter: by looking at high levels of electromagnetic energy alone, we are ignoring other potential intermediary forces, which although we cannot directly produce, our consciousness can still avail of. Low-energy systems, such as human thoughts and concentration, can avail of the mysterious forces of the cosmos and use them as interfaces to affect change on the other end of the process. The high-energy system of material science simply blasts right through them, while operating in ranges where low-energy systems are non-detectable by them. Mainstream science appears to exclusively view energy—in terms of any generation and transmission—as high-energy output and consumption processes. If we scale down the overall effects to one of low-energy, the potentials and possibilities of the electromagnetic spectrum remain the same. Humans are low-energy transmitters and receivers. We are no different in this respect from most of the biological processes which occur on this planet.

This low-energy system, so to speak, was how our ancient ancestors had a very different relationship with the megalithic stones they held as sacred. They did not need mega-volts, kilowatts and multi-amperage current. The sorcery was in the subtle nature of the electromagnetic environment. Indications are that the *Dark Matter/Energy* mystery is also a low-energy phenomenon. Therefore, we are already hard-wired through our biology into the largest power source in the cosmos. From the electromagnetic forces of the human mind and body, and into the realm of what is disparagingly called *Dark Matter/Energy*—or some other as yet little understood aspect of the *Quantum* effect—to create, change, or alter the outcome at the other end of the process. Once again, we do not need to completely quantify—nor fully understand—the intricate complexities of these systems in order for us to benefit from their value. As a friend of mine once told me, after she was once cured of a severe rash by a local *Folk Magic* practitioner when conventional medicine had failed to alleviate the issue, "It only works if you **believe** it works." At this point in the text, it may be worth pointing out that there is something of a comic irony, in that the largest and most high-energy consumption machine on the planet—the *Hadron Particle Collider*—exists so as to uncover the most low-energy particles in the universe. If this does not tell us something about materialist science, then nothing will. Eventually, all roads lead back to sorcery, even the ones which seek to deny its existence.

CATALYTIC EXTERIORIZATION PHENOMENON

In April 1909, the Swiss psychoanalyst Carl Jung was visiting the father of psychiatry, Sigmund Freud, in Vienna, when the two began something of a heated argument after Jung had brought up the topics of precognition and parapsychology. Freud began to demonstrate great condescension towards his younger protégé. During this heated exchange, Jung felt a strange sensation within his diaphragm. With this, a large heavy bookcase in the room began to bang violently for no apparent reason. Jung turned to Freud and announced, "There is an example of a so-called *catalytic exteriorization phenomenon*!" When Freud discounted such an idea, Jung announced he would do it again, and another loud bang took place within the bookcase.

For the rest of his life, Jung was unable to explain to himself and others what had caused him to perform this feat, apart from being able to give it a name. He chose to just accept what took place in the bookcase as proof of the limitations of Freud's materialistic views, and considered it as a personal validation that the human body could indeed manifest and affect forces outside of itself. There is no doubt that the experience also deeply disturbed Freud, if his letters are anything to go by. Rather than give credence to the possibility that Jung's 'occultism' ideas may be worth exploring further, Freud resigned himself to explaining the event away as creaking noises in the old woodwork, which just happened to occur while himself and Jung were debating. Modern debunking had been born.

Yet what Jung had demonstrated in Freud's office has been reported by people all over the world. Drinking glasses suddenly exploding by themselves during moments of extreme emotional tension, for example. Mothers being able to lift cars off of their trapped child, and so on. In the days when people still brought their electronic equipment to be repaired, there were some technicians who could 'fix' a radio or TV without so much as removing the screws to get access to the interior. I personally knew one of these electronic mystics myself. It was as if he could make the electrons move once again through the circuit board, merely by being in close contact with it.

QUARTZ, ELECTRONICS AND SOUL MEASUREMENT

This same natural ability to repair broken electronic and electro-mechanical equipment has also been demonstrated by individuals who can make a watch—which had stopped working—begin ticking again by the act of holding it in their hands, as the quartz inside the watch suddenly becomes charged once again. The quartz timepiece itself was developed at Bell Telephone Laboratories in 1927, when it was discovered that quartz is a *piezoelectric* material which will accumulate an electrical charge when exterior forces impact upon it (sound familiar?). The signal can be held, driven (flexed) and resonated by the quartz crystal. In other words, quartz can acquire, hold and then transmit electromagnetic information. Suddenly, our ancient ancestors and their relationship towards sacred stones does not seem so primitive after all. Especially when one factors in the strange and seemingly inexplicable cultural fad of the '*Pet Rock*', which arrived in the aftermath of the quartz hand watch. In the mid 1970s, the most modern humans were once again venerating sacred stones.

What technicians and engineers were calling the 'quartz revolution' of the 1970s had been already known by the builders of the ancient—and quartz-laden—stone megaliths as well as by the promoters of *Psychometry* (measuring the soul), such as Joseph Rodes Buchanan, who coined the term in 1842. Psychometrists believe that stones contain actual memories of the events—which they have been witness to—and that these memories can be played back into the minds of people with the ability to receive them. In this respect, I tend to differ from this viewpoint, as I am more inclined to agree with Philip S. Callahan in his book, *Nature's Silent Music*, that this effect is most likely caused by the subtle diamagnetism effects of these stones activating sequestered tribal associations and memories within a certain individual's DNA.

THE BODY ELECTRONIC

During my formal study of electronic engineering at college, I recall one lab experiment involving all the students building something called a *High Pass Filter.* This is a circuit device which avails of a phenomena known as *attenuation*—and is designed to reduce signal frequencies. Everyone in the class built the same circuitry—using the exact same components—to the same design. The lecturer then tested each circuit on an *oscilloscope.* All the students in the class—who had correctly built the circuit—achieved the same result, within an acceptable range of tolerance common with analog electronic components of the era. That is, except, for my finished project. The *High Pass Filter* which I had built measured a completely different level of attenuation than the rest of the class. Although I had built the circuit correctly—according to the text book— my result was very different. We checked the components for faults, such as incorrectly marked resistors, mislabeled capacitors, and so on. They were all fine. The lecturer laughed and made some good-natured comments about me having super powers. For good reason, I kept my mouth shut and was happy with the passing grade. At the same time, I was also practicing magical rituals as outlined in various books I had been reading at the time. In particular, David Conway's book *Magic: An Occult Primer,* which has been a huge influence on me since my early teens. I could practically recite entire sections of it by heart, and I had performed most of the magical experiments in the book. Until that point, I was assuming that I was not doing it properly, as no outstanding results had been achieved with my magical rituals and practices. However, the *High Pass Filter* experience—which was to be repeated in other lab experiments—was something of a validation for me that I was becoming more 'magical'. It proved beyond doubt that our thoughts and psychic states can indeed affect the electromagnetic spectrum—directly—via an interface of some mysterious forces operating between our minds and the objects or devices in question.

As far as I was concerned, from that point on, sorcery was not only real, but I was now capable of doing it. After all, my magical abilities had been scientifically lab-verified by an *oscilloscope*! Within a few months, I had dropped out of college and never bothered with my formal electronic studies ever again. I became increasingly drawn towards the arts from that point on. Initially music, and then painting. It was almost as if something in me had initially generated my interest in electronics purely as a means of validating my experimentation into magical practice later on. Sorcery is ironic and poetic, if nothing else.

THE SIGIL

During my formal study into electronic engineering at college, I became acutely aware of the startling visual similarity between what is known as magical *Sigils* and electronic schematic diagrams. The shapes, arrangements and overall designs were remarkably similar. Many of the shapes familiar to the occultists of the past would be, in the field of electronics, recognizable as the symbols for diodes, vacuum tubes, antennas and potentiometers to any student or designer of analog electronic circuits. The process for the controlling, amplification, trimming and directing of electronic current within the symbols/components of an electronic circuit, a *Sigil* performs much the same thing, with a flow of psychic energy. It is a compression, manipulation and containment of forces.

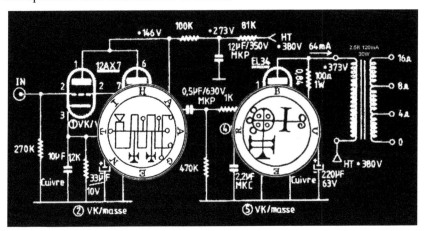

The first *Sigils*—and even, to an extent, *piezoelectric* devices—were the cave and rock art symbols of the Paleolithic, Neolithic and Bronze Ages. Carved design elements such as concentric circles and wavy lines were born out of specific desires to amplify the electromagnetic qualities already present within these quartz-laden 'sacred' stones of our ancestors.

In an age without electro-smog, our ancestors would have been far more sensitive to faint electrical charges and fluctuations contained within certain stones and rock croppings, which modern humans today—in most cases—are unable to detect. The proliferation of quartz outcroppings and seams being so prevalent at megalithic stone sites attests to this. In many ways, these were the world's first crystal radios, and what Braun, Marconi, Tesla and Bell perfected during the great age of radio and electrical pioneering were simply a continuation of what the shamans, and later druids of the megalithic cultures had begun thousands of years previously.

The Bohea Stone in County Mayo, Ireland is a classic example of a magical outcropping, with its scores of rock art designs carved into its surface. Each design is fine tuning the electrical charge created by the massive quartz seam at its base. Even today, it is not hard to envision a Neolithic shaman, standing atop the natural platform on the Bohea Stone, chanting in the direction of the stars—or the setting/rising sun—while surrounded by hundreds of people, perhaps each rubbing two pieces of quartz together in unison with the magical invocation. The sparks they produced—by the electrical charge inherent in the quartz—lights up the twilight vista of the landscape, while also illuminating the psychic vista of each and every person present. The shaman or druid chanting—perhaps in celestial salutation—as he or she becomes the focus of this collective charge, so as to project their consciousness into other realms and dimensions of space and time. Another similarity between sorcery, the early days of radio development, and that of ancient rock art symbolism is the desire to communicate with non-human entities for information about the future, or to gain information about life beyond the human mortal existence. The early days of radio development were never far from the *Spiritualism* movement of the same era, availing of the on-going improvement and sensitivity of electronic and electrical components as a means to contact 'spirits'. For all we know, this technical refinement and research into radio broadcast and transmission may well have been conducted 'at both ends', so to speak, suggesting the possibility that these same 'spirits' were as eager to work with the development of radio as much as the mortal scientists and hobbyists were —on this side of the veil—attempting to communicate with them.

Neolithic and Bronze Age rock art would appear to be connected to similar ideas of connecting with and consulting other entities outside human perception. In Scandinavian folklore, the rock art represented by cup or scoop marks—a common design feature on megalithic rock art worldwide—were used to make offerings of seeds to the fairies or elves in the hope that a reciprocation of some kind (almost certainly magical) would be granted. The first pre-Nuragic Neolithic culture of Sardinia was consumed with these ideas, and entire geological complexes and outcroppings were carved into them, as well as altered in order to create what are known as *Domus de Janas,* or 'fairy houses'. These complexes were developed entirely for the purpose of confronting and communicating with other entities. Many of the stylized human petrographic representations—found at Neolithic sites from Sardinia to Siberia—may well indeed be portrayals of what we today call 'demons'. In Russia, for example, within the Cape Bosov Nos region, a landscape of fantastical rock art interpretations of these entities can be found along a vast region from north of Saint Petersburg to the *Arctic Circle*. They are openly referred to as 'demons'—but not necessarily in the 'evil' Christian sense—and are generally surrounded with what appears to be rock art *Sigils* designed to attract these demons. In all cases, we can see that the modality of creating, and then 'switching on' a magical device—from a megalithic structure to a magical *Sigil*—and on to the early days of radio technology, the same overall process is in action:

1. a desired intention of outcome to influence unseen forces.
2. an object or device which will create and focus the available present forces into a focused and manageable form.
3. a mysterious medium in the guise of these unseen forces, spirits, demons, fairies—or the consciousness of a shamanic individual —who will act as a courier or interface.
4. evaluating and continually refining the outcome through repetitive and regular enactments—often connected with cosmological cycles—of the ritual itself.

As we can see, sorcery is not so very different than the scientific methods that were utilized during the days of *Natural Philosophy*. We still see this today in the high-tech world of particle super-colliders where sub-atomic elements are fired into highly controlled environments in order to manifest a '*god particle*', or some other mysterious and unknown force from beyond. Intention and focus of the available forces (and devices) are key to the successful outcome of the desire. However, due to the relative nature of such ideas—regardless of any or all technical and other exacting specifications—we can't measure the outcome of the design of *Sigils*, *Talismans*, spells or rituals with the same tolerances we can apply to, say, engineering. It's always going to be a shot in the dark. A shot, however, in the general direction of the target or outcome.

DILIGENCE IN SPELL MAKING

As previously mentioned, what makes this such an interesting exercise—specifically within the practice of sorcery—is that the end result is often poetic and surprising. Your desire may be born out of greed in wanting a million dollars so as to give you power over others. However, you might acquire that million dollars as a result of a terrible accident which leaves you paralyzed and you win a law suit or insurance payout. So be careful. When practicing all sorcery, maintain a modest and achievable aim relevant to your present life and social situation. As countless Dennis Wheatley novels have warned us, when the British aristocrats became so megalomaniacal in their belief that they could rule or 'improve' the world using their sorcery, bad hexes always came back to them in equal measure to their intention. The end results were never pleasant for them. Likewise, the fate of the magically-paranoid Romanov royal family—and eventually, how this impacted upon Russia itself for a century afterwards —demonstrates succinctly that sorcery operates at the level you are playing at. So aim low, and aim true, and then cherish the outcome, no matter what that is.

HOW TO DESIGN AN EFFECTIVE AND SAFE SIGIL

All magical and supernatural experiences—which we are personally subjected to—are electrical at the point of physical origin (our nervous system and neurology). The 'tingling sensation' is the most common effect which most people notice. This is still a relatively little understood sensation, and one which occurs during heightened states of awareness. What we do know is that the experience has been determined to be electrical in nature. Adrenaline literally 'fires' the neurotransmitters. This is the origin of the charge.

The deep emotionality of the experience is also what literally shoots this force out of our bodies into the environment around us. We get goosebumps—as well as the hairs on the back of our necks standing on edge—as this charge exits our physical bodies. Unfortunately, no studies on how this charge functions in tandem with the body's aura have ever been undertaken. However, I suspect that it plays a part in the overall 'shunting' effect which allows the *Will* to eventually impact upon exterior targets. A magician will deliberately generate this charge by means of concentration of *Will*, sexual (including masturbation) or other heightened sense of awareness methods (drumming, dancing, etc.). I know of one magician who creates their *Sigil*, and then takes a roller coaster ride. All during the experience, he stares at the *Sigil* to focus the charge into it. This is an excellent method of powering a *Sigil*. Others use the momentum of aircraft taking off and landing. Skydiving, rock concert mosh pits, and bungee jumping have all been utilized. Even intense combat or dangerous wartime situations have had their charge driven into a *Sigil*. London, during *The Blitz* of 1940, was a hotbed of occultism for this very reason.

By purposeful amplification of our internal psychic-electrical properties —and by means of amplification of this charge—we can project our consciousness beyond our physical bodies. This is not dissimilar to how a song on the radio is being transported—beyond the station transmitter— inside a carrier wave being broadcast by a high-voltage electrical discharge into the surrounding atmosphere. However, to harness this charge effectively into a *Sigil* is to literally seal a deal with the cosmos. Again, this is a low-energy process and hence, why the results are never instantaneous, as the likes of *Harry Potter* would have us believe. A magical process is a seed being planted into non-material soil and fertilized by your *Will*. All seeds need time to grow and eventually flower. As previously mentioned, the successful outcome depends crucially upon the focus and compression of the *Will* towards that desired outcome. This literally fertilizes the *Sigil*. In order to achieve this desired outcome, we can create a *Sigil* towards that end.

Sigils are a relatively modern method in terms of popular usage. Derived from ancient magical *Seals* and reinvented by Austin Osman Spare during the early twentieth century. They are, nonetheless, the most effective—and accessible—system yet devised for manifesting our desires or *Will*. This also accounts for their growing popularity. *Sigils* are simple, and can also be an individual artistic expression in terms of how you wish to create and modify the design. They appeal to our personality and sense of design and style. We feel comfortable in creating them. They are *The Art* in totality.

In the past, other similar processes existed in the form of Finnish knotted ropes, Viking *Runes*, Irish *Ogham* script, *Kameas* (magic squares), as well as the Hindu *Yantra*. All would have been used to charge the intention into the creation of the symbols or text. This was, and still remains, a common form of sorcery all over the world in numerous cultures. The *Sigil*, within modern Western sorcery, has become the de-facto method of transforming intention into desired outcome. This is why numerous corporate logos are the most common forms of *Sigil* sorcery we see today. Because they work. It must also be pointed out that the longevity of the *Sigil* as a working method is rather surprising. Eventually, one method of sorcery will supersede the previous method. Yet the *Sigil* itself has remained remarkably effective and resilient. Even so, the *Sigil* will, in time, lose its power and be replaced by another method. Memes on social media, as well as cryptic anonymous riddles on Internet message forums, are showing great promise in this regard. Nonetheless, the *Sigil* still reigns supreme for now.

THE POWER FORCE WITHIN THE LINES

Symbols not only have meanings; they also have power. A logo for a specific restaurant chain not only tells you their offerings, but will also cause you to salivate and become hungry when you are not. The associations have been created between your biology and the psychic transmission of the logo. This is still sorcery; however, it is *Trash Magic,* using sorcery for the most crude and base forms and desires, mainly manipulating others subconsciously or against their own *Will*.

In the past, the *Sigil* (in the form of a *Seal*) was a pictorial representation of a demon, and was central to the practices of demonology as well as ceremonial sorcery. The *Seal* achieved great popularity during the European *Renaissance,* although the general premise and concept, as we have seen, goes back to at least the Paleolithic era and perhaps even before this. In the Middle Ages, *Sigils* (*Seals*) were also used to invoke the favors of what were termed angels, and also to summon demons.

However, even if these terms and identities were effectively a means of naming and identifying with specific unknown forces, there are still hierarchical approaches to doing this. Remember that we 'invoke' an angel, god or other higher power. We 'summon' demons as servants. Never attempt to impose your demands upon a god or angelic being if you invoke one deliberately, or do it by accident. A very powerful and life-changing accidental invocation happened to me when the Egyptian god Sobek manifested in full form at the end of my hospital bed. I was going through incredibly painful and emotional trauma in the aftermath of a major operation. Towering over seven feet high, Sobek's crocodile head glanced down upon me with casual, dismissive contempt. When you are in the presence of a god, you'll know it. Sobek was telling me to get my own life together and stop feeling sorry for myself. As Sobek is also a god strongly connected to *Apotropaic Magic,* I was also being informed that I had protection from any forces which might seek to harm me. No words were exchanged. The gestures of a god are more than enough.

At the risk of continually laboring the point, just because we can summon a demon, or invoke a god or angel, it is not necessarily wise to absolutely state that these archetypes/entities are real beings, as such. There is always a fine line between an archetype and an actual god. They almost certainly appear to be real when we encounter them. At the very least, they are profoundly intertwined with our own deep inner consciousness. The ancient Greeks referred to this as being *Chthonic,* and is believed to have been derived from much older Pagan cults in the Balkan region. They invented a whole pantheon of deities and archetypes to underpin this hidden aspect of the earthly realm, or underworld (as being symbolic of the psyche), and which was to later make its way into analytical psychology. With the arrival of *Chaos Magic* in the 1970s, an almost iconoclastic, irreverent reaction to ceremonial sorcery was unleashed— which sought to modernize the *Sigil*—and to bring ritual up to date with emerging social, cultural, as well as technological trends. What makes the *Chaos* approach to *Sigil* making so appealing is the individuality of the design. Along with the less formal approach, this attitude towards the *Sigil* takes the idea somewhat back-to-basics as a kind of modern *Folk Magic* practice, giving sorcery back to the masses.

When making a *Sigil*, the use of language is vital. Therefore, **any desire of the *Will* is written in past tense so as to imply that it has already manifested**. Remember, the desire has already taken place, and you (in a psychic sense) have to get out of the way so it comes into manifestation. So asking or requesting is something of an interruption—if not destruction—of the magical intention. It is also important to dispel notions of present space-time, and instead, project the consciousness into the future, and, if necessary, also into the past.

Firstly, we shall begin with the desire. In this example, a desire to produce a healthy and productive garden. Therefore, we shall word the intention as thus:

MY GARDEN WAS FRUITFUL THIS SUMMER

Assuming this is being written in the springtime, notice how our consciousness has already been projected into the future towards the satisfactory outcome. An outcome which has already happened. In the psychic future, so to speak. We are already directing the *Will* in a very powerful manner, simply by losing any sense of possibility or chance in terms of how we approach the desire. Next, we remove all the vowels, and we are left with this:

MY G RD N W S FR TF L TH S S MM R

Now remove the repeating consonants:

MY G RD N W S F T L H

These become the letters from which we will form our *Sigil*. There is a school of thought that the initial request itself must be made up of as few words as possible. This is an arbitrary assumption. State your desire in a manner you feel comfortable with.

STYLISTIC CONSIDERATIONS

There are a number of varying and personal approaches to do this. The important point is to attempt to make the *Sigil* as pleasing to one's eye as possible. When making *Chaos* sigilization, it is important to remind yourself that there are no hard and fast rules. The vast majority of both ancient and modern sorcery is intuitive and personal in nature, and therefore, subject to customization and adaptability, while also taking note of methods that have been successful in the past.

I myself tend to enlarge the first letter. Some people would consider the letters 'M' and 'W' as being similar in terms of overall design, and will combine them into a single 'hybrid' letter. This helps to compress the design. In the case where a sizable amount of letters is to be sigilized—as in this example—I would suggest doing this. In a case where there are, say, less than six letters remaining after you have removed the vowels and repeating consonants, in this instance, I would use all these letters. Another technique I have found to be effective is using the letter 'Z' rather than 'S', as per the American manner of spelling certain words. The letter 'Z'—for whatever reason—seems to be innate with a more 'active' nature than the 'S'. Its basic shape also tends to sit better within the construction of *Sigils*.

Please note: **I did not create a *Sigil* based on this example, as it might actually be dangerous to myself.** Remember what I stated at the start of the book about privacy of one's magical workings are to be kept secretive and out of prying eyes? There are numerous books and websites dealing with the stylistic construction of *Sigils*—which include final examples—that the reader can avail of.

A PERSONAL APPROACH TO THE ART

Again, I am demonstrating a personal technique which has worked for me. You can also develop your own approach, as sorcery, like any art, is open to interpretation and improvisation within the framework of well-tested and established methodologies. One thing I will stress, however, is that in order to prevent any outside harmful forces attracting themselves to the *Sigil*—and thereby your future outcome—I always place a strong and stylized border around the *Sigil*. This also makes the overall aesthetic aspects of the design seem pleasing and complete.

I tend to take this one step further, by drawing a field of radiating curved and pointed patterns surrounding the *Sigil*. This is inspired directly by the *Chaosphere*—a symbol of eight radiating arrows from a central point developed by Michael Moorcock—expressed in a more free-flowing and organic manner. The same idea can be seen in the likes of Celtic border designs around sacred manuscripts, and so on. Again, this serves to illustrate the personal, interpretive nature of the *Sigil* within sorcery. Although the general trend is to compress and minimalize the letters into a compact form, I have found that, for me personally, a more artistically flowing approach suited my personality. More Klimt than Kandinsky, while something else entirely may be more suited to your own take on the subject.

We must never lose sight of the fact that sorcery is an art. In the past, practitioners of *Folk Magic* would have to make use of what was available to them. While today, magicians can avail of computer mainframes and data sets to generate complex *algorithms* if they so wish. It is no different than a making a piece of art from a few twigs and branches bound together, or creating an *IMAX CGI* movie. It's still art, and whatever your taste in art represents will generally be reflected in how you choose to practice your sorcery.

Example of Icelandic *Sigils*, known as '*Staves*'. Used in Iceland from 1100AD to the present. Their origin may have been derived from the first Irish and Norwegian settlers who arrived in Iceland with their own methods of *Folk Magic*, developing into a new magical hybrid. This demonstrates how sorcery adapts to changes in social and cultural circumstances as they arise.

ON CURSES
AND CURSING

I often surprise people when I tell them that I hold the idea of cursing in very high regard. Although this may seem—on the surface at least—to be a rather strange statement, let me explain further. The very idea of cursing another person or group comes with something of a built-in safety mechanism which can cause the curse to backfire upon the person who issued the curse. If the curse is issued without justifiable cause or reason, the consequences of casting an unwarranted curse or hex upon another person puts such endeavors outside the pale of superficial parlor games and infantile revenge fantasies. Play dangerous games, win dangerous prizes.

We live in an age whereby every discount store witch hat-wearing mage and magi are cursing people whom they do not like based on often imaginary—or histrionic and infantile—grievances, undertaken in order to overcome a sense of powerlessness which they are burdened with as individuals. First and foremost, this feeling of powerlessness is something that really needs to be confronted and dealt with by the individual issuing the curse. Attempting to transfer this burden onto another person—even if completely justified—should be the last option. See a therapist before picking up your wand, if this is your prime motivator. The path to a successful magical life is constant self-analysis and self-reflection. Those who are driven by impulse and hysteria are a danger to themselves and others when they dabble in the magical arts.

In the vast majority of these instant-revenge 'curses', nothing comes to pass in terms of the curse affecting the target. However, in some highly psychologically-charged individuals, and who are not of balanced mind, for whatever reason, can generate a colossal charge towards the target only for the curse to come 'charging' back at them with often appalling consequences. I have seen this actually destroy several people, and I have known of one person in this situation where it cost a woman her own life. Suicide can sometimes result from a rebounded and unjustified curse. **Curses always work to some degree. Who it is that the curse ultimately affects is the main area of consideration in this regard.**

In February 2017, a global 'magical' movement—of mostly role playing hysterical adults—collectively embarked upon cursing U.S. President Donald Trump, in what they called a *mass binding spell*. The farcical nature of the *Harry Potter*-type cosplay fiasco should have been hilarious if not for the fact that myself and others soon realized that the entire event was probably orchestrated by some dark occultist—so as to ride the charge created by the *mass binding spell*—for their own purposes. Not only did the curse have no effect on the U.S. President, but the dollar store witchy-poos who took part in the event will be the ones left to deal with the energetic rebound. A lot of sleepless nights and 3AM terrors as their reward. If they get off lightly.

A true magician would casually consider the politically-dogmatic, arm-wringing turmoil—created by the Trump election—as the unleashing of new charges and potentials to be captured and to be utilized accordingly. You can't fight *City Hall*. Instead, you can ignore 'the resistance', and then enjoy the mass stupidity of others letting themselves be tormented by it for your own amusement. Rather than letting large scale political forces crush you—by trying to make you think you can change what you never can—see it as a potential power source. Barring this, satire and bardic sorcery will never go out of fashion.

SO YOU WANT TO MESS UP ANOTHER PERSON'S LIFE?

The bottom line regarding cursing is: don't do it (as a rule). Or, at least, wait until you are on your death bed—or have reached rock bottom in your life—with little or no chance of escaping from your hardship. Conversely, if you are the victim of genuine malice and injustice, there is a fool-proof means of going about this in 'relative' safety. It's still risky, but less so. As the method behind this type of curse will not satisfy any pathological hunger—not to mention instant gratification—of unstable revenge-obsessed individuals, they are unlikely to be interested in utilizing this method of cursing. This type of curse only works if the individual—being a truly deserving target—walks 'into the trap', so to speak. Before I demonstrate this foolproof method of cursing another person, allow me to reinforce the dangers and ethical consequences, so it is clear in the reader's mind.

Ultimately, we are talking about the sabotaging of, and then reclaiming of one's life force or psychic energy. If the individual whom you are cursing did not intend you any personal harm, then they generally won't pay any energetic price. However, if the person making the curse is behaving immaturely, infantile, hateful—and without good reason for cursing the other party—then it will be the sorcerer's own life energy which will be depleted. In some cases, this also opens the door for entities which will attach themselves to the malicious individual who cursed an undeserving person. The psychiatric hospitals of the world are filled with these types, who played with an unwarranted fire which they could not contain.

CURSES CAN TRAVEL IN FAMILIES

Also bear in mind that, like the *Banshee* of Irish folklore, curses can pass down through the family line from generation to generation. Therefore, on to innocent people who will not have deserved this. Women cursing their ex-spouses, for instance, might find that the child they had with the father—whom they have cursed—develops a painful illness or psychiatric condition. In the past, when someone referred to themselves, another individual, or a family as being 'cursed', it could be meant very literally. They may have been cursed at some point in the past. Hence, why this section of the book comes with an extreme cautionary warning. This is not a game for the idiotic or the infantile.

A BRIEF HISTORY OF CURSING

Before we get to the finer points of cursing, it is worth looking over some examples of famous curses from the past. Cursing on a large scale was common among the Pagan Anglo Saxons and the Irish Gaelic tribes of the past. Within the *Irish Mythological Cycle*, Amergin Glúingel, the powerful druid of the Milesians Gaels (not to be confused with the philosophical school of ancient Greece), issued forth a powerful curse in the form of a bardic satire towards the Tuatha Dé Danann. This led to the deaths of their three most powerful kings, and the loss of their control over Ireland. Amergin—by means of an epic bardic poetic verse—charged his whole being with the mass-energy potential of the very essence of Ireland in order to attain revenge for the wicked murder of Íth. The curse was so powerful that the Tuatha Dé Danann—as a race—paid a heavy price, which eventually would banish them from the face of the earth and into the inner world. One of the oldest forms of cursing found all over the world is what popular culture has come to term as being the *Voodoo Doll*. The origins of this form of sorcery go back at least as far as ancient Babylon. In Europe, the body shape of the target was fashioned from spent candle wax. Pins made from hawthorn branches would be stuck into the doll as symbolic energetic daggers. The popularity of the waxen image was assured, mainly due to its impressive aesthetic and psychological nature. The curse required almost no skill or real commitment on the part of the practitioner.

Popularity aside—in more cases than not—the pierced doll curse would result in failure to cause the target any harm. In the rare instances when the intended outcome was successful, it might result in the sad and slow deterioration of the target over a number of years. By then, the individual who initiated the curse would have probably forgotten about the person they cursed, and in most cases, moved on with their lives. There is an important realization in this which sadly is lost on far too many who rush to the craft store to buy fabric, modeling clay and dressmaker's pins. Ultimately, the desire for immediate revenge loses its novelty, and from this, any energetic recovery desired by the magical practitioner would be piecemeal at best.

Proficient cursing, which results in successful hexing of the target, is a serious art form which takes genuine skill, patience and courage. In energetic terms, it is going into battle with sword in hand. The potential risks are as serious as the possible results. The expert and erudite use of language plays a major part in issuing forth an effective curse. The practitioner must be of balanced and stable mental fortitude, with a strong sense of personal intuition and innate wisdom.

When these personality traits are coupled with a curse cast by such a person, it becomes an extremely serious matter. Only patience and creative intelligence can deliver the required result without the danger of magical rebound or energetic blow-back. Competent and wise practitioners will often issue their curses—openly targeted towards a specific individual(s)—as their life is coming to an end, having nothing more to lose in material or health terms. The person being cursed will generally live out the rest of their days in a state of constant despondency and hopelessness. The star within them is almost extinguished to the point where death becomes a welcomed respite from their unending sense of dread and eternal unease.

During the *Medieval* period, when the Normans ruled much of Ireland, there was one famous case of an archer who attempted to blow out the eternal fire venerating the goddess Bríd at her shrine in County Kildare. Soon afterwards—subject to a curse placed upon him for this act of sacrilege—the records report that the Norman archer became insane and attempted to blow out every other fire he saw. Eventually, he died of a combination of heat exposure and dehydration, after his comrades attempted in vain to save his life. We can observe, in this case, how the outcome of the curse was poetic and ironic in nature, considering how the curse eventually manifested.

SOCIAL DAMAGE AS A RESULT OF CURSES

The use of curses in rural Ireland—along with the real or imagined effects upon the cursed—would sometimes result in the target attempting to bury themselves alive in their own homes by lifting up the floor slabs and digging their own symbolic graves which they would lie down in until they died. Old Ireland—as with most agrarian cultures in Europe— would have been saturated with witchcraft, sorcery and curses. Both casting and repelling. This would have been an everyday part of life.

In such societies, the curse would generally take the form of hexing the livestock and, therefore, economic security of the target. Cows would stop producing milk, hens would stop laying eggs and crops would not grow, and so on. The house I myself live in, here in rural county Sligo, once belonged to a witch in the 19th century who had cursed the well which served the local community. Apparently, she was a Protestant lady and the community was mostly Catholic. Sectarian tensions at the time led to this unfortunate situation. This serves to illustrate that sorcery was —at one time—a form of warfare among rural peasant families and communities. Not only in Ireland, but all over Europe and beyond. These rustic energy wars resulted in communities dealing with the aftermath of inter-generational cursing and hexing. Emigration usually was the only option left to escape a curse or hex. Sometimes, this rural energy war would be brought to the new country, as demonstrated by German peasants in Pennsylvania continuing the magical conflict started on the other side of the Atlantic.

The most effective curses take a considerable amount of effort to create, and their results occur over a long time frame. Remember, we are dealing with the unknown forces of the universe when we embark upon magical practice. These forces are not subject to the same space-time effects as that in which our own day-to-day cognition operates. Among the peoples of the *Scottish Highlands,* a long magical tradition—coupled with something of a historical magical charge inherent in these communities— has, in the past, led to some very effective cursing that resulted in the entire destruction of several clans over the course of time. Most notably, the Houses of Seaforth, Mar and Mackintosh.

Indeed, so feared were the witches and sorcery of Scotland, that the most influential individuals of that land made use of powerful *Talismans* and *Lucks* as something of a magical firewall against any possible curses. It is no coincidence that William Shakespeare's *Weird Sisters* became the most infamous witches in Western culture, based on their unforgettable appearance in *Macbeth.* These three witch sisters in the '*Scottish Play*' are representative of the same magical archetype as the *Three Fates* in Greek mythology, and the *Norns* of Norse mythology. Fictional they may be, but, but nevertheless, Shakespeare based them on real accounts of Irish and Scottish witches as described in *Holinshed's Chronicles* (1587).

Such was the power of the *Scottish Highland* witch, that very real fears of their sorcery was almost certainly the reason for King James VI of Scotland's writing his highly influential *Daemonologie.* A book—along with the notorious *Malleus Maleficarum* (*Hammer of the Witches*)—that became something of a mandate for the vicious persecution of witchcraft practitioners for centuries to come. Further back in Scottish history, Robert the Bruce at the *Battle of Bannockburn* (1314) carried with him a polished crystal as protection against any sorcery coming from the English side. These protective gemstones and *Talismans*—which are still employed in the jewels of the British and other monarchist bloodlines— offer protection against all manner of sorcery and curses. Once again, we see that while the ordinary lay person is told to laugh at and ridicule the idea of curses, the ruling classes continue to the take the idea of being cursed very seriously.

The social and cultural aftermath of a society or community consumed with cursing can be both catastrophic and enduring. If you wish to roll this dice, you best make sure you deserve to be at the gambling table. You, and more importantly, people who may have done you no intentional harm, can lose literally everything.

LET THE CURSING BEGIN

Which brings us to the 'safest' method of cursing. Firstly, we are dealing with your personal psychic energy having been stolen by a pathological individual. Matters not if this was a financial swindle, an act of unwarranted slanders, emotional or sexual abuse; it still all comes down to energetic forces being stolen, regardless of the material or psychic form they represent. As previously mentioned, a potent process is to lay a type of magical trap for the cursed to walk themselves into.

Say, perhaps, someone is attempting to ruin your reputation by means of scandal or a smear campaign. The most effective method for the practitioner—to assure that this injustice is avenged in the form of a curse —is to issue the text of the curse publicly on, say, social media, and then wait for the provisionally cursed to find out about it and hopefully proceed to mock it. Even though you mentioned no name when you wrote the curse, the target (in their own narcissistic self-destruction) will assume it was aimed at them. Thereby, their mocking or ridiculing of the curse will attach it upon their being. In effect, they curse themselves.

Such a method ensures—to as an effective degree as possible—that the curse will not rebound upon the practitioner, due to the fact that it did not originate (as such) from the magician, having mentioned no 'named target' within the wording of the text. The provisionally cursed—after assuming the curse was directed at them and then publicly mocking it—

will have bound themselves up in something comparable to an energetic trap. A trap made of energetic barbed wire from which there is no escape. Be warned: this will be a heavy burden for the practitioners who partook in this hex that they will have to live with. So make sure that the curse is fully justified before making it. An example of the type of wording used in this kind of curse is shown thus:

I WILL, TO HAVE STOLEN THE SUN FROM THEIR MORN, THE DREAMS FROM THEIR HEART, THE LOVE OF THEIR KIN, THE VIGOR OF THEIR FORMS, THE CHARGE FROM THEIR DESIRE, THE TASTE FROM THEIR MOUTH, THE FIRE FROM THEIR WANT AND LEAVE SOLITARY THE MALIGNANT LIE WITHIN THEIR VISCERA AS THE ONLY COMFORT AND COMPANY AMONG THE COLD AND ISOLATION IN A WORLD THAT CHERISHES THEM NOT.

You can see how a poetic play on words creates an effective sense of emotionalism and drama when read aloud. As this methodology is rooted in the bardic and satirical sorcery of the druids, we are talking about an ancient form of literal 'spelling' which has stood the test of time. The more one has a tendency to be articulate and erudite, the more effective one's sorcery will be. This is not to say that a practitioner needs to be a master of language or a spellbinding wordsmith in order to cast and repel effective curses. However, it does help. There are other methods which can be employed, such as humor. Magic is called *The Art* for a reason. Do not—at the same time—become overly verbose by indulging in word salad. State what needs to be stated and no more.

THE LAST RESORT AND AVOIDING REGRET

In most cases—with the passing of time—personal reflection or compassion overrides this desire of the practitioner to seek revenge. In most cases, decent people will carefully consider the full potentiality of any curse they were planning. In many ways, this is the greatest path a magician can take with their craft. To attain a level of wisdom and self-awareness—within the course of their magical existence—so as to simply 'be' at peace with the prevailing order of the world. Having moved beyond a 'win'/'lose' orientation and, instead, allowing the mysterious forces of the universe to take care of the accounting complexities.

Sorcery is at its most powerful and effective when it is modest and unassuming. The greatest magicians who have ever lived would hardly stand out from the crowd if they walked down any street in the world. By contrast, look at the effort, regalia and constant vigilance required to keep the sorcery of the royal families in power. How very unlike the woman in the *Strength Tarot* card, who calmly and so easily tames the power of the mighty lion. There is our magical, psychological and spiritual role model: the goddess *Forteza Virtus* portraying the most sublime and inspiring image of the skilled sorcerer.

MAGICAL SYMBOLISM AND GEOMETRIC SORCERY

Sorcery—within the present era—is ultimately a science of language concerned with stripping down language into its base components to the point where it becomes practically indistinguishable from symbols. This is what James Joyce was attempting within Molly Bloom's soliloquy (while she is masturbating) at the end of *Ulysses,* as well as that of her dreaming within the surreal follow-up novel, *Finnegan's Wake.* The rolling and merging of syllables into oratory *Sigils* by means of reading the text aloud. We often forget that humans are completely capable of functioning and operating as a society by means of the use of symbols alone. Once, that is, we are privy to the conventions of the actual symbols themselves. Symbols representing the compression of complex ideas and messages into minimum space and basic shapes. Within the lexicon of symbols, the negative spaces are as vital as the lines and shapes they are encapsulated by. Try to imagine musical notes without the pauses. The opening chords of Beethoven's *Fifth Symphony* being a good example of how such specific punctuation adds to the emotional impact of the piece.

During our journey into the world of sorcery, it is important that we first begin along this path by developing a symbolic, or geometric literacy (I despise the term '*sacred geometry*'). Our earliest ancestors realized that in order to explain the unseen dynamics of the cosmos, making basic geometric shapes—starting with the circle—was the most effective method of both visualizing, and then building up their cosmological model of reality. This was an extremely effective idea which has stood the test of time, and why it remains so central within Freemasonry, even to this day.

I see no reason to change this approach, as it has worked for thousands of years and is still a very effective tool. Sorcery is very much about reconstructing one's own reality model by using the basic building blocks provided by the universe. The use of geometry in creating a shift in consciousness—so as to allow the unseen forces of the cosmos to enter into a more effective dialog with your subconscious mind—is a universal method most people can grasp, regardless of culture or education level.

As the human subconscious mind is far older than the conscious mind, the subconscious communicates by means of symbols and shapes. Our brains also generate shapes—without an exterior light source—which are known as *phosphenes.* These shapes conform to many of the symbols we see on the rock and cave art of our earliest ancestors. By understanding and defining these concepts—using geometric and symbolic shapes—it also allows us to bypass the gatekeeper standing guard over our often educated, egotistical and narcissistic modern cognition. A cognition which thinks it knows it all. So for this reason alone, the use of symbol literacy in the 21st century is perhaps more vital than ever.

The graphic of the six-pointed *Hexagram* (within a circle) will be used to illustrate the ideas in this chapter. As most people have been conditioned to see this graphic as something of a static model, I have deliberately added the noise effect to the black background—in and around the image —so as to give it a sense of vibration and movement. This is to represent the unseen forces of the cosmos. In certain cultures, this background field is sometimes represented by the rippling primeval waters, or as the fluid within the womb.

Adding this sense of vibrating undercurrent to these ideas is also why the *Impressionist* painters worked with short brushstrokes. Eventually allowing Vincent van Gogh's *Starry Night* to predict the soon-to-emerge field of *Quantum Physics,* by taking the ideas of Monet and Seurat to the next level. Van Gogh's sad life story is also a damning indication of just how lost we have become in the West since the *Enlightenment.* A time when we began to isolate our mystics—while they are alive—so they could be celebrated as visionaries after they have been slaughtered by their own hands, or by that of another. Sadly, Prometheus still has to steal the fire of the gods, as they still won't give it up without a fight.

Think of this graphic as being akin to a color wheel on the first day at art or graphic design college. There are hundreds of books and websites dealing with the formation and construction of geometric forms in order to demonstrate the dynamics of the universe. I am not going to repeat them all here in order to make the spine of this book thicker. I chose this particular graphic because it contains enough of the basic elements for the purpose of illustrating the overall point I am making within this chapter. Meditate upon what you see above. Within it lies the entire cosmos and everything contained within the entire cosmos.

TRANSCENDING SYMBOL ILLITERACY

Symbol illiteracy is a two-fold issue for many people today, as it allows corporations to construct logos that can spellbind the masses into purchasing their products. While religion and the present *Bible Belt*-nature of the post-unreconstructed conspiracy world has cultivated pointless—if not extremely damaging—fears and paranoia within some people who have been taken in by that scene. Sadly, without them applying a measured and critical analysis of the mostly bogus (and hysterical) information they are being sold concerning symbolism. If you want a definition of 'black sorcery', then robbing people of their conscious development by means of cultivating fear and ignorance surrounding the *All-Seeing Eye* and so on, would be it.

THE POINT AT THE CENTER

At the center of the symbol where the two diagonal lines meet within the illustration is, put simply, the beginning of all creation. From the underlying chaos of dancing sub-atomic particles vibrating within the cosmos—what the ancient Egyptians call the *Nun*—we can take a pin and stick it onto any one of them. At this point, we have brought the universe into existence. Congratulations; you have the makings of becoming a god or goddess. Don't get carried away, though, as we still have some way to go. However, your consciousness has pinned itself to this one mysterious and unknowable particle. Now you can do something with it. This is the seed of the *Yggdrasil World Tree*, the tree of the Norse mythology, or the sacred oak tree acorn of the druids. The point at the center of the *Rose Cross* flower. So what next?

Here is an idea: you can stick a compass point into it. "What is the nature of this compass?" I hear you ask. Well, it's your consciousness. That has always existed and always shall. As you are able to perceive—and then isolate this one point in the universe—you are also able to do this only because you are aware of the universe to begin with. Therefore, your consciousness is capable of evaluating and comparing different parts of this universe in relation to, and apart from, another part of this universe.

This is also why the Freemasons use the symbol of the compass on their insignia. It is represented in Egyptian mythology as the arc of ejaculated semen issuing forth from the phallus of Atum. So, we have pinned the needle part of the compass on this one point. Now we can open up the compass and put the other end on another point in the universe. Then one becomes the two. You have taken the first step into creating a universe of your own. Just as the god Atum brought himself into manifestation.

THE OUTER CIRCLE

Now begins the important part. Using either of the two points we have pinned down, let's now draw a circle. This then creates the boundary surrounding the graphic as a whole. The magical circle. The demarcation frontier between the known and the exterior untamed regions beyond the circumference. Along with this, all the creative and magical potentials are waiting for us within the circle itself. In symbolic terms, this is represented by the *Fool* card in the *Tarot* taking his first step into consciousness. All the other cards within the *Major Arcana* could be placed along the interior circumference of this circle until we return once again to the *Fool*.

We are now aware of cycles and orbital motions. The modern depiction of *The Fool* is based upon a *Medieval* illustration by Giotto (above), in which he suitably illustrated *The Fool* as almost shaman-looking in appearance. That is what *The Fool* in the *Tarot* actually represents: a shaman about to embark on a mystical journey into an unknown cosmos of his own creation. However, his journey is guided by the underlying mechanics of the material universe which unfold—in symbiotic tandem —with the unseen forces of consciousness and *Dark Matter/Energy* which generates it all. It cannot be stressed enough how important the creation of the circle is within the scheme of human consciousness development and creative exploration.

Look again at the hexagram graphic and keep moving your attention around the circle and in both directions. Consider the eternal nature of the circumference. There is no beginning and no end. Rather than being trapped with a flat plane, we can now begin to visualize the two-dimensional circle as a helix which has been collapsed like a *Slinky* toy straight out of the box.

By projecting the concept of the circle upwards and downwards, we now have opened a portal of sorts, moving in two directions. It becomes an endless spinning path through space and time. The stone circle builders of the Neolithic and Bronze Age would have first marked out their circular formations—as lines on the grass or sand— to then later place larger boulders around the circumference so as to project the two-dimensional circle on the ground into three-dimensional space.

Everything in the cosmos manifests itself out from arcs, circles and spirals.

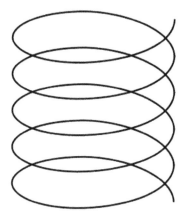

We see these stone circles all over the world—as if they are born from some primal human instinct—in order to understand and convey this experience with the generative forces of both circles and spirals, as with the recent discoveries in France of Neanderthal circles.

Found deep within cave systems created by removing stalactites—from the roofs of caves—and then placing them into a circle on the cave floor, the mysteries of the circle and the spiral have been recognized and pondered by our very earliest ancestors. Before humans had a fully developed language, when we still were barely distinguishable from other primates, we began to create art and symbols in order to generate magical ideas, and the very first of all of these was the circle, and from this, the spiral.

This also found its way into sound, with the circular drum. Shamans do not have square or rectangular drums for this reason. The circle became the womb from which human consciousness developed. The universality of this idea covers the entire globe, and remains as an idea across a vast time-span of human existence. In Ireland alone, it is estimated that there are possibly forty thousand circular embankment enclosures known as 'raths' or 'fairy forts'. There are four of these 'fairy forts' within a short walking distance of my house. The magical circle was the primal infrastructure of human existence for thousands of years. In many ways, we created ourselves as a species from out of the magical circle.

Now that we have projected the circle upwards and downwards as a helix, we become aware that, by looking into the circle (from above), the helix tapers off into the distance in the form of a spiral. This now forms the shape of the *Cosmic Egg*. The circle can be visualized as a snake coiled around the egg—holding its tail within its mouth—when seen from above. This is the *Ouroboros* of the ancient Egyptian and Greek mythological and spiritual traditions, which is also represented—in a more developed form—by *The World Serpent Jörmungandr* of the Norse mythology, who encircles the entire planet.

In all cases, the image represents the circular and perpetual nature of creation and the forces contained therein. A universe of purposeful destruction and rebirth in which there is no beginning and no end. We do not have to concern ourselves with keeping the universe functioning, as the process is self-maintaining and self-regulating. The circle, as visualized as a cross-section of this cosmic world, or *Orphic Egg,* is common to the mythology of many spiritual traditions around the world.

It represents the unborn potentials of all that will manifest from within it. The 'Big Bang' of cosmology—created, incidentally, by a Jesuit priest—is essentially a modern pseudo-secular interpretation of the same idea. An idea so powerful than even science can't do away with it. In Chinese mythology, the heroes were often depicted as breaking out from an egg. To the alchemists of the Middle Ages, the egg represented a symbol of perfection as the *Prima Materia* from which the *Alchemical Fire* hatched. The yolk was the symbolic gold, while the white was the symbolic silver.

Now that we can begin to understand what can be generated from this universe, we can now draw intersecting lines and divide the circle into the quadrants of the *Celtic Cross*, or the Tibetan *Mandala* if we so wish. Pull the central point upwards—from where the cross hairs meet—and generate a cone. Draw a square within the circle. Grab the central point where the diagonal lines of the square intersect. Remember now; you are becoming a god so you can do this. Now pull it forward to create a pyramid from within the square. Rotate the square within the circle and this creates a cube. All of this by means of simply drawing lines within the initial circle you created. As the complexity emerges and evolves, we still are subject to the geometric possibilities—and, to a degree, even the limitations—of the design by keeping the shape uniform and pleasing to the eye. It is up to our conscious mind to meditate upon and contemplate the meaning of the geometric shapes and imagine what we can do with them. These shapes are pleasing to the human eye. What do they tell us? They conform with the natural world and common ratios we are familiar with. Where you take it to—once you have mastered the basic idea—is up to you.

THE HEXAGON

Let's return to the circumference of the circle again. By drawing six equally spaced points along the circle, then connecting them to one another, we can now create a *Hexagon*. We can rotate the circle and, with it, the *Hexagon* inside it. Or, we can move them independently of one another. Look again at the full graphic at the start of this section, and imagine the interior shapes rotating within a sphere around the central point, similar to that of a gyroscope. Let your mind do this, and observe the dynamics of the universe in all their motion expressed by this idea. They are all there: hydro-thermal, nuclear, and electro-mechanical energy. From the hunter-gatherer rubbing two sticks together to start a fire, to the theoretical physicist pressing the start button on the *Hadron Collider,* it's all contained within this simple idea. But what's making it all move? The answer is: **you**. Your imagination and creativity. You are moving it. Your consciousness, in tandem with the unseen forces representing the ninety five percent of the universe—that scientists can't find—is moving it.

There are numerous other shapes we could have placed within the circle other than a *Hexagon*. I chose the *Hexagon* for this exercise, as there is something visually and proportionally pleasing about this particular design when placed within a circle. It is also beautifully demonstrated by the hexagonal-shaped storm atop the northern polar regions of the planet Saturn. Even more amazingly, within the center of Saturn's polar *Hexagon* is a powerful and mysterious vortex.

If we look at the planet Saturn from above, its outer ring, the polar *Hexagon*, along with the swirling vortex at its center, it functions as something of a real-time cosmological example of the concepts I am describing here. We may even be witnessing Saturn still in the process of its own creation. Generating itself from out of the terrifying and convulsive chaotic abyss. Generating and devouring its own recycled elemental forces. Forces billowing out from its gaseous mass, and all contained within the magic circle of its famous rings. In *Alchemy*, the *Scythe of Saturn* symbolizes that he is the god of both harvest and time, represented by the element of *Lead*, being the merciless entropy and decay necessary for new life.

Within Islamic mysticism—which itself was originally derived from the Yemenite lunar worshiping Pagan tribes of the Arabian peninsula—the *Hexagon* represents an important step up from the *Pentagon,* which precedes the *Hexagon* by amalgamating the five elements of the five-pointed star (*aether,* fire, air, water and earth). This then resolves itself into material bodies via the six movements of the *Hexagon* within the circle. As it generates—up, down, forward, backward, moving left and right—we now have the basic building blocks of biological life, creatures, entities, humans, animals, angels and demons. Now let us connect all the points of the hexagon together and create a soul to reside within it. The inside star.

THE SIX-POINTED STAR

By connecting the points of the *Hexagon,* we create the *Hexagram* by means of the two overlapping equilateral triangles. The creative conjunction of opposites. A familiar shape popularly known today as the *Star of David,* and one which has become synonymous with the Jewish religion and the state of Israel. Although the six-pointed star can indeed be found within ancient Hebrew texts, its popularity came to greater prominence among Jews living in the *Pale of Settlement,* an imperial region of western Russia which existed between 1791 and 1917. Prior to this, some Jewish communities in central Europe were already using the *Hexagram* symbol on religious texts and on their buildings. It was not until 1897 that the *First Zionist Congress* chose the symbol as a central, unifying insignia for world Jewry. From then on, the shape became universally known as the *Star of David* or the *Seal of Solomon*.

Nevertheless, the *Hexagram* was already a very powerful symbol in both religion and the occult long before this. Having fist derived—along with the *Swastika*, another powerful symbol—within the Vedic and Buddhist traditions of the Indian subcontinent as the foundation of the *Sri Yantra* mystical diagram.

Although rudimentary and primitive versions of the design have been found all over the planet, it is also possible that an original Pagan Neolithic structure—which inspired the Jews to settle in Bohemia—may have contained a simplistic, rock art *Hexagram,* which the first rabbis on the scene perhaps interpreted to be an ancient synagogue from the time of the *First Temple* in Jerusalem. It is also important to note that the Bohemia Jewish tradition is one steeped in magic and astrology.

The universal power of the *Hexagram* symbol is that it allows one to easily visualize the connection between the material and non-material worlds. Creation and manifestation of life. In Hinduism, the two overlapping equilateral triangles are seen as the *Linga* (phallus) entering the *Yoni* (vagina) and therefore, the symbol presents a powerful creative and self-replicating force of unified opposites: male-female, light-darkness, polar opposites, and so on. This is where the 'soul' of the symbol comes into its own. The reason why this is so important is due to the two offset equilateral triangles. Despite being sympathetic and equally proportional with one another, they are not perfectly overlapping. They are set apart, and this leads to the concept of the gray areas between absolutes.

We are now in the domain of moving, undulating frequencies and cycles. The gyroscope within the sphere is no longer trapped spinning and rotating at one particular place in the cosmos where it was manifested. It can now also move the sphere away from the initial dot—from which the initial compass point was created—and on towards its own conscious desires so as to explore and create. There is also no absolute within the smaller *Hexagram*—which we created by making the six-pointed star— and now we can create another six-pointed star and then another inside it.

Again and again, into and out of the wormhole of infinity. Novelty is now in effect. We have uniqueness and personalities. Our *Will* is in charge now. There are no limitations. Sorcery is born.

This exercise can be applied to any concept or intention whereby imagination can be manifested into a material form or process. What works for an artist—imagining a fantastical landscape within their minds and painting it—will also work for a magician hacking the building blocks of the cosmos. It's ultimately the same thing. However, it does not come about merely by imagining and visualizing the outcome alone. The 'work' has to be undertaken to make it so. The use of geometry as a means of expressing, as well as tapping into cosmic forces, was beautifully demonstrated by John Dee, with the *Sigillum Dei Aemaeth* (below). Initially derived from a late Middle Ages magical amulet, it is designed to attain power over all beings and entities except *Archangels*.

The *Tantric Mandala* of the meditation deity, *Vajrayogini*. Her invocation provides methods for transforming aspects of mundane human existence into paths towards enlightenment. She is situated at the center of a *Pentagram*, demonstrating the embodiment of all cosmic forces within the ordinary life of a human being. *Vajrayogini* allows transformation beyond the mortal and towards one's personal godhood.

ON DARK OCCULTISM

Black Magic practice—as with all the occult arts—is very real. Regardless of whether people want to believe it is not. It is most certainly very real to the hundreds of thousands of people worldwide—and in your community—who practice, or have been victims of the *Left Hand Path*. Did the *Son of Sam* serial killings—which took place in New York City during the 1970s—not actually occur because David Berkowitz was a member of a murderous dark cult performing rituals in a park just north of the Bronx? Rituals of animal sacrifice and invoking demons, which in time caused a city of ten million souls to live in fear and panic?

Tell the victims of David Berkowitz and their surviving family members that *Black Magic* isn't real. A vast modern metropolis was paralyzed with fear and dread. Such manifestations of the dark arts should be seen in terms of a certain type of artistic performance designed so as to viscerally affect the intended target(s). *Shock Art* comes directly from *Black Magic*. While the absurd circus troupe family of Anton LaVey may seem comical to our eyes today, back in the 1960s, much of *Middle America* was literally petrified in terror by his farcical *Church of Satan.*

As British occultist Francis (X) King so eloquently stated on the subject of all sorcery;

> *"The motivating power, then, in all magical operations, is the trained* Will *of the magician. All the adjuncts of Ceremonial sorcery—lights, colors, circles, triangles, perfumes—are merely aids to concentrating the* Will *of the magician into a blazing stream of pure energy."*

So therefore, everything from propaganda to smear campaigns can be considered forms of dark occultism. The menacing figure in a hooded black robe standing in the center of a *Pentagram* surrounded by a circle. Or the teenagers in a cemetery at night, invoking the power of their 'satanic majesty' are not the be-all-and-end-all of dark occult sorcery. Mostly it's just a sad joke. However, sometimes it is very real.

It all depends on the *Will* of the dark magician and how effectively and easily his or her concentration can be harnessed and directed. Likewise, do not be expecting your local *Black Magic* practitioner to be wearing a black cape and making sinister gestures in your general direction. They are also using their 'invisibility' too. Very often, he is either the charming, refined gentleman, or the 'harmless' lady in the supermarket. At least Roma gypsies give us visual indications of who they are, and what they are capable of doing to us—with their own brand of sorcery—if we insult or offend them. The most effective forms of *Black Magic* come from the most mundane, average-looking citizens.

However, and on a more sobering note, it is important to consider that dark sorcery often achieves powerful results much more quickly—and with less effort—than 'white' sorcery in the hands of a skilled and adept individual or coven. These are the psychic attackers who will arrive as charming gentlemen bearing gifts and compliments, while the monster's real intention—underneath the delightful and polite surface—has been harnessed and camouflaged. This is how mind-control cults function. They arrive into your life bearing promises of salvation at a time you need this the most. This is also *Black Magic* in action. Make no mistake.

Think of the fictional residents of the *Dakota Building* in New York as portrayed in the Roman Polanski movie *Rosemary's Baby*. They arrived as compassionate and caring neighbors. Eventually, Rosemary unknowingly undergoes an incremental and appalling psychic attack. She is subjected to endless *gaslighting,* as well as being tormented by strange and terrifying dreams, and her neighbors are a ceremonial *Black Magic* coven in cahoots with her psychopathically ambitious 'perfect' husband. The perfect partner, who was using his young wife—as a kind of human battery hen—for a demonic entity to mate with, so as to advance his own acting career. In fact, the deterioration of the character Rosemary in the movie—as played by Mia Farrow—is an excellent cinematic portrayal of a person undergoing a psychic attack, or the result of a successful curse. That is precisely how the experience appears to a concerned friend or family member looking on: mental confusion, poor health and signs of mania.

HOW SAFE ARE WE?

Without attempting to overly concern the reader, we have to contend that even in this day and age, someone using dark sorcery upon us (however unlikely) could be a real possibility. Access to occult knowledge and materials from the 1960s onward—including the growth of cults and covens—has created a situation whereby we have to come to terms with the fact that anyone wishing to become skilled in the use of *Black Magic* can develop this pathological occultism, courtesy of the endless tools and resources at their disposal.

The irony being that in this—the age of the *Internet*—we are more likely to encounter a skilled occultist than our distant ancestors in the Middle Ages may have fallen foul of. Often, we are very surprised—and not in a pleasant way by any means—to discover that a co-worker, social club member, church group associate, love rival, difficult neighbor or even a member of our own family is a secret adept of the black arts. You could find yourself being the one in the path of their carefully directed 'blazing stream of pure (malicious) energy'.

Take comfort in the fact that one is not commonly going to be a target of a black magician unless you have something they really want, or you have deeply offended them somehow. **However, you most certainly will be a target if you have you have threatened to expose their activities to the general public.** This would be a most unwise thing to do. If you suspect they are involved in criminal activities, then keep your mouth shut and file an anonymous complaint with the police. Otherwise, stay out of their path.

Part of the rites of a *Black Magic* ritual is always to announce their intention to the target beforehand. So, no matter how subtle the warning, you had better take heed of it and do not try to play the hero. Sometimes it can be in the guise of a gift, such as a book. **Which is why you should never accept gifts from people whom you hardly know.** Make sure to not bring them into your living space unless you have come to fully trust them outside of your home. If you have mistakenly taken a gift from a person whom you suspect may be using it to place their malevolent energetic force(s) into your home, then burn it in a fire and dispose of the ashes in a fast-moving stream or river. Protect your living space with salts, quartz and constant burning of good quality incense. These safeguards make it far more difficult for the malevolent psychic force to enter into the sanctity of your home. Organic sea salt, in particular, disrupts and dissipates the dark sorcery.

THE CACODAEMON AND THE DJINN

The primary initial indicator that you are being psychically attacked by a black occultist—rather than extreme jealousy from a malicious individual—is that you have a constant sensation that you are being watched all the time. This feeling is ever-present, as in some cases, the magician—as incredible as this sounds—has created a type of slave entity to do this.

This specific type of *Fetch*—which is a seemingly living thought form—can appear as an animal; often a bird, or even a black, sometimes human shape, in the corner of one's vision. Other times as a floating and swirling dark mist above the target's bed at night. The ancient Pagan Greeks termed these entities *Cacodaemon,* which has even been incorporated into modern psychology as the condition known as *cacodemomania.* This is when a person believes that they are being tormented by an evil spirit. Which is precisely what is taking place.

The purpose of the *Cacodaemon* is to try and intensify the target's anguish and fears further: by compounding the intensity of the psychic attack. The legendary *Foo Fighters*—the balls of light—which harassed *Allied* aircraft during the latter days of the *Second World War,* may well have been similar thought forms created by the many occultists operating within the *Third Reich*. Or perhaps even by the sheer desperation of the population of Berlin and their almost messianic belief in a *'Wonder Weapon'*, which they may have subconsciously unleashed in the hope of saving Germany from defeat at the last moment. In the Islamic world, the *Cacodaemon* is known as a djinn (Islamic non-human form of consciousness), and wizards use these plasma entities to attack a person from a place outside of human perception and senses. Certainly, in the Islamic world, the concept of the djinn is still taken very seriously, even among educated people.

For this level of psychic attack to take place, it is entirely dependent upon the black magician to have either a lock of the target's hair, the sexual energy of the target, or to have left an object with the target. This 'gift' is what the entity uses as a kind of homing device to locate the target having already been made familiar with it. *Invisible Ink* is sometimes used to create a *Seal* on the cover of a book, made with something as common as heavily diluted cola-based soft drinks.

Along with books and cards/letters, this gift can also be a piece of jewelry (diamonds are very effective djinn carriers) which had been previously 'charged' by the black occultist with the specific purpose of an entity under their control being able to locate the object to torment the target. In the case where you cannot burn the object, instead, place it inside a sealed bottle or jar, and throw the object into the sea or a lake.

Make sure it is weighed down. The bottle or jar isolates the object from the water, which it can still use to find its way back to the target. Demons don't drown. Make sure the jar or bottle containing the object sinks, by tying it to a brick or similar heavy object. To remain at the bottom of the ocean where the black magician cannot retrieve it for use on another person. In doing this, you may be also protecting other people from future harm. This is also why our Viking, Gaelic and Anglo Saxon ancestors threw objects that they believed to be 'cursed'—such as bent swords, axes and coins—into rivers, lakes and the sea.

Even people who were executed for the most horrific crimes—such as pedophilia—were thrown into the stagnant peat bogs so they could not reincarnate. It was also considered to be something of a votive offering to the peat bog; the deeper the body of water, the safer everyone was from evil men reincarnating. In *Vedic* mythology, there are several legends surrounding deities performing this act of preventing reincarnation among the wicked; such as Krishna decapitating the heads of evil demons —regenerating from the blood pouring out of the wounds of the giant Andhaka—using his *Sudarshana Chakra* as a flying discus, so they would be prohibited from reincarnating into a new body. Same rule applies for a 'cursed' object. Discarded and forgotten. This was also the metaphor and inspiration for J.R.R. Tolkien's character of the hobbit named Sméagol, accidentally discovering the submerged *One Ring*. Created by Sauron the Dark Lord, it could be used to psychically attack and corrupt anyone who possessed it. Some things which are lost are best left lost to the world.

PSYCHIC ATTACKS AS PASSIVE CURSES

The majority of people who engage in psychic attacks are—to put it crudely—jealous and uncultured morons (or people of highly limited world views). In the vast majority of these psychic attack cases, this is what one will be dealing with. Humans beings—at this stage in our cultural, social and evolutionary development—appear to be far more capable of achieving intense levels of hatred much more easily than we are of intense levels of compassion and understanding. Such intense levels of pathological psychic activation can do great damage to people on the receiving end.

Putting a curse (psychic attack) upon another person (unknowingly or knowingly) is far easier for some people than accepting that they might not be as beautiful, skilled, dynamic or likable than their object of hate. This malicious and pathological demographic represents a percentage of the population greater than most people are willing to accept. Such individuals should be considered as being something akin to *Passive Black Magicians*. If you have ever felt yourself under psychic attack, then these are these same types of people who—in all probability—have placed you under a psychic attack, or have the potential to do so. One is also no less in danger from a psychic attack in a small town or rural community than one would be in a large town or city.

Please bear in mind that this final section of the book is not about making the reader paranoid. There are precautions and safeguards we can incorporate into our lives so as to protect us from being the target of such malicious energy wars. Chances are, most of you reading this may never have to deal with this situation. However, being prepared against this possibility is something I would still strongly recommend you consider seriously. The protection of your magic circle is the primary concern when we embark on the path of sorcery. Thankfully, there are proven tools and methods which we can avail of.

SHUNGITE SORCERY

In the year 1293, the *Third Swedish Crusade* into Finland—in what is today northwest Russia—was launched with the sole intention of finally exterminating the Pagan Karelians once and for all. At the time, it was one of the last major regions/ethnic cultures in Europe to resist the expansion of Christianity. The *Third Swedish Crusade* was part of the overall *Northern Crusades* against Pagan communities on the southern and eastern shores of the Baltic Sea. Genocide, coercion, brutal domination and forced baptisms of indigenous Baltic, Finnic and Western Slavic peoples were central to this military campaign. Soon after the crusade was completed, a romantic narrative of holy missionaries peacefully bringing the *Gospels* to the region was invented, in order to completely exterminate the previous Pagan cultural and tribal associations of the region. This historical revisionism wiped out thousands of years of culture and spirituality. This is not so much cursing an individual, but entire tribes; robbing them of what they used to be, so the Catholic Church could make them what they needed them to be. This came from the Roman military culture of absolute *conquest.*

As a result of this cultural and spiritual annihilation, along with the subsequent persecutions that would last several hundreds of years, many Karelian Pagans continued to practice their non-Christian beliefs and customs underground and out of sight of the Pope's swordsmen. The previous Pagan gods venerated by the Karelians—such as their equivalent of the thunder god Thor, called Ukko, as well as the sea god Ahti, and the woodland deity Tapio (who shares the same archetypal attributes as the *Green Man* of the Indo-European tradition)—were culturally converted into mere folklore and superstition. Which, ironically, is probably what preserved their memory for future generations.

As time passed, the reputation of the 'witchcraft' of the Karelians only grew in stature, as many northern Europeans began to seek out these Finnish 'witches' for the kind of supernatural help which the *Gospels* and rosary beads could not provide them with. Amid endless, and on-going persecution, the paganism of the Karelians—as well as other forms of Finnish witchcraft—became the primary form of magical practice across a vast region ranging from Russia to the North Sea.

As the Karelian witches traveled throughout northern Europe, they brought with them a strange coal-like black stone—which could only be found in rural outposts known as Shunga—on the shores of Lake Putkozero, in what is now Russia. The black stone which these witches carried was known to have great power, as well as being strangely mesmerizing to hold and examine, and which today we know as *Shungite*. The healing properties provided by the black stone of the Finnish witches was first officially sanctioned by none other than *Peter the Great,* who created a spa in Karelia in order to make use of the purifying nature of the mysterious black slate.

My own experience with *Shungite* is relatively recent, and I can attest to its awesome power. The nature of the *Shungite* molecule is its ability to literally capture and retain not only other minerals and electromagnetic effects, but also seemingly human and other forms of consciousness. A common magical use I have developed with *Shungite* is to hold the stone in the palm of my hand and pour all my intentions into it and then place the piece of *Shungite* into a river. To date, the results yielded have been quite spectacular, leaving me in no doubt that *Shungite* is a remarkable stone fully deserving of its growing reputation. As water is the easiest substance for the collection and dissemination of human consciousness, I am using *Sigil* magic less these days, preferring *Shungite* sorcery instead, for the purpose of manifesting my desires. The potential of this remarkable, mainly carbon, mineraloid black rock—in both magical and healing potentials—will only increase in reputation and scope. Bring it into your life, in its raw, unpolished form. Cherish and charge it, and *Shungite* will protect and present its power to you willingly.

SALT MAGIC

Another mineral vital in the practice of magic and sorcery is sea salt, especially the organic flakes of salt from the Dead Sea in Israel. During the 1980s—while I was living and playing music in New York City—a friend of mine from Hong Kong had the 'ghosts' in his old apartment removed by his mother using a Chinese method of throwing large flakes of sea salt-infused rice around the rooms, in the belief that the salt could capture the ghosts. The salt flakes and rice grains—now containing the ghosts—would be swept up, placed into a paper bag and thrown into the Hudson River.

Salt should also be placed in a small pouch or sock and carried with you at all times if you feel you are under psychic attack from a malevolent individual or entity. Sleep with the pouch or sock of organic sea salt under your pillow. Although a word of caution concerning the energetic absorption of salt: it should be noted when practicing your own magic rituals, that salt can absorb this energy too, so it is more effective as a barrier against unwarranted energetic intrusions during complex rituals. It stays outside the magic circle.

IN CLOSING

During the course of this book, I have purposely avoided presenting the reader with a complex tome on the practice of—as well as any complex knowledge concerning the topics of—sorcery. There are, quite literally, thousands of such books already in print to teach you this, should you wish to take it a step further. Rather, I have laid out my overall personal philosophy on the general approach to the subject with the aim of presenting useful information that also functions as something akin to a tactical handbook on the topic of sorcery.

Along with this, I hope to have made the point that there is—and always has been—a real magical class system in effect. A class system, whereby the most powerful people on the planet are aware of certain aspects of reality which can be changed/manipulated in accordance with *Will*. This knowledge gives them an extreme advantage over the rest of us. In some ways, by having read this book you are now something of a dangerous man or woman.

However, you are also a much safer man or woman. There are times I shudder to think what may have happened to me following that entity attack in Sardinia, had I not been aware of the power of cold, salt water baths as a means of destroying my attractiveness as a nest for a particularly powerful entity. Sorcery has not only made my own life more interesting, creative and fulfilling. It has saved my life on occasion, too.

Think of this book as something of a manifesto for magical equality. You now have the information, and hopefully your life will be safer and more rewarding as a result of having *Sorcery: the Invocation of Strangeness* within your personal possession. The world will become a very different place for you from this point onward. You will find that you are less subject to the forces of personal, social and cultural challenges which arise in your life. Now you have the means to alter not only how they affect you, but to change the outcome in accordance with your *Will*.

Thomas Sheridan
Sligo, Ireland
Imbolc, 2018

ALSO BY THOMAS SHERIDAN

This book sets out to examine the wider concept of magic and mythology being utilized as an early form of social psychoanalysis by the druids, and how magic theory and occult symbolism developed from this. How this evolution of ritual magic eventually made its way into folklore, witchcraft and freemasonry. From the proto-shamanic world of the megalith builders, to the lost civilizations of the Atlantic fringe, along with the continual changes and challenges to the human experience in the face of traumatic cultural upheaval, the druids and their legacy have played a far more influential role than has been previously acknowledged. *The Druid Code: Magic, Megaliths and Mythology* utilizes folklore connected to sacred sites, developing a bidirectional conduit back through time, to reveal what took place in 2500BC. A shift in human consciousness that made humans what we are today. From Atlantis to alchemy, you will never see history and mythology in the same way again.